China Briefing, 1981

Also of Interest

*China Briefing, 1980, edited by Robert B. Oxnam and Richard C. Bush

*China's Economic Development: Growth and Structural Change, Chu-yuan Cheng

Technology, Politics, and Society in China, Rudi Volti

Technology, Defense, and External Relations in China, 1975-1978, Harry G. Gelber

Military Power and Policy in Asian States: China, India, Japan, edited by Onkar Marwah and Jonathan D. Pollack

Perspectives on a Changing China: Essays in Honor of Professor C. Martin Wilbur, edited by Joshua A. Fogel and William T. Rowe

China's Quest for Independence: Policy Evolution in the 1970s, edited by Thomas Fingar and the Stanford Journal of International Studies

*China, the Soviet Union, and the West: Strategic and Political Dimensions for the 1980s, edited by Douglas T. Stuart and William T. Tow

*China: A Political History, 1917-1980 (fully revised and updated), Richard C. Thornton

The People's Republic of China: A Handbook, edited by Harold C. Hinton

*China's Four Modernizations: The New Technological Revolution, edited by Richard Baum

Urban Development in Modern China, edited by Laurence J. C. Ma and Edward W. Hanten

*The Chinese Military System: An Organizational Study of the Chinese People's Liberation Army, Second Edition, Revised and Updated, Harvey W. Nelsen

*China in World Affairs: The Foreign Policy of the P.R.C. Since 1970, Golam W. Choudhury

*Available in hardcover and paperback.

About the Book and Editors

China Briefing, 1981
edited by Robert B. Oxnam and Richard C. Bush

As China begins the 1980s, it faces perplexing questions, both old and new: Will the system that has evolved since 1949 accept daring political and economic reforms? Can the Chinese leadership end, once and for all, the contentious debate over the Cultural Revolution and the leadership of Mao Zedong? Can it strengthen currently frayed bonds of loyalty between a battered state and a skeptical society? What will a new administration in Washington mean to U.S.-China relations? These and other questions are addressed by China specialists in *China Briefing, 1981*, prepared by the China Council of The Asia Society. The annual's up-to-date reviews of the crucial issues facing China today will be of interest to all China watchers.

Robert B. Oxnam, now president of The Asia Society, directed the Society's China Council in 1975-1981 and its Washington Center in 1979-1981. Among his publications are *Ruling from Horseback*, *Dragon and Eagle* (coedited with Michel Oksenberg), and *China Briefing, 1980* (coedited with Richard C. Bush).

Richard C. Bush is program associate of The Asia Society's China Council and Washington Center. He is coeditor (with Robert Oxnam) of *China Briefing, 1980*, and is co-compiler (with James Townsend) of *The People's Republic of China: A Basic Handbook*.

China Briefing, 1981

edited by
Robert B. Oxnam
and Richard C. Bush

Published in Cooperation with the
China Council of The Asia Society, Inc.

Westview Press / Boulder, Colorado

All rights reserved. No part of this publication may be reproduced or transmitted in any form or by any means, electronic or mechanical, including photocopy, recording, or any information storage and retrieval system, without permission in writing from the publisher.

Copyright © 1981 by The Asia Society, Inc.

Published in 1981 in the United States of America by
    Westview Press, Inc.
    5500 Central Avenue
    Boulder, Colorado 80301
    Frederick A. Praeger, Publisher

Library of Congress Cataloging in Publication Data
Main entry under title:
China briefing, 1981.
    Includes index.
    1. China--History--1976-   --Addresses, essays, lectures. I. Oxnam, Robert B. II. Bush, Richard Clarence, 1947-
DS779.2.C442   951.05'8   81-12973
ISBN 0-86531-256-7   AACR2
ISBN 0-86531-257-5 (pbk.)

Composition for this book was provided by the editors.
Printed and bound in the United States of America.

Contents

About the Contributors   ix
Foreword, Irv Drasnin.   xi
Acknowledgements xiii
A Note on Romanization   xv
Map of China xvii

1 INTRODUCTION.   1
   Robert B. Oxnam

2 THE RISE OF HU YAOBANG AND THE PROBLEMS OF
   ONE-PARTY RULE.   7
   Richard C. Bush

3 FROM FEUDAL PATRIARCHY TO RULE OF LAW: CHINESE
   POLITICS IN 1980.   17
   Richard Baum

4 THE CHINESE ECONOMY IN 1980: DEATH OF REFORM?   41
   Bruce L. Reynolds

5 YOUTH IN CHINA TODAY: OBSTACLE TO ECONOMIC
   MODERNIZATION?.   53
   Thomas B. Gold

6 CHINESE FAMILIES AND THE FOUR MODERNIZATIONS. .   67
   Deborah Davis-Friedmann

7 US-CHINA RELATIONS IN 1980   79
   John Bryan Starr

APPENDIX A: BIOGRAPHICAL SKETCHES OF MEMBERS OF
   THE POLITBURO OF THE CHINESE COMMUNIST
   PARTY   93

APPENDIX B: DOCUMENTS ON US-CHINA RELATIONS . . .   107

   The Shanghai Communique, February 27, 1972. . .   107

Normalization of US-China Relations,
December 15-16, 1978. 109
Taiwan Relations Act of 1979. 111
Statement of Secretary of State Haig on US
China Policy, March 16, 1981. 114

APPENDIX C: A STATISTICAL PROFILE OF CHINESE
ECONOMIC DEVELOPMENT. 115

INDEX. 117

About the Contributors

Richard Baum is professor of political science at the University of California, Los Angeles. He received his doctorate in Chinese politics from the University of California, Berkeley in 1970, and has written widely on China's politics and modernization. Most recently he was editor of China's Four Modernizations: The New Technological Revolution, published by Westview Press in 1980.

Richard C. Bush is a program associate of The Asia Society's China Council and Washington Center. He studied Chinese politics at Columbia University. He is coeditor (with Robert Oxnam) of China Briefing, 1980, and co-compiler (with James Townsend) of The People's Republic of China: A Basic Handbook.

Deborah Davis-Friedmann is a professor of sociology at Yale University. She did her graduate work at Boston University and Harvard University, specializing on the elderly in Chinese society. She did field work in both Hong Kong and China, where she was one of the first American scholars to do research since 1949. The results of her research will be published in Long Life: Aging and Old Age in the People's Republic of China, forthcoming in 1982.

Thomas B. Gold is a Harvard-trained sociologist. He was an exchange student at Fudan University in Shanghai from early 1979 to early 1980 (he has also studied in Taiwan). He has interpreted for a number of high-level Chinese delegations visiting the United States, and is currently completing his doctoral thesis on the economic development of Taiwan.

Robert B. Oxnam is president of The Asia Society. He directed The Society's China Council from 1975-81 and its Washington Center from 1979-81. He received his doctorate in Chinese history from Yale University. Among his publications are *Ruling from Horseback, Dragon and Eagle* (coedited with Michel Oksenberg), and *China Briefing, 1980* (coedited with Richard Bush).

Bruce L. Reynolds is professor of economics at Union College in Schenectady, New York. He holds a doctorate from the University of Michigan, and has published many articles on the Chinese economy. He did research in China during the first half of 1981.

John Bryan Starr did his graduate work at the University of California at Berkeley, where he subsequently taught for six years. His doctoral dissertation was published in 1979, under the title *Continuing the Revolution: The Political Thought of Mao*. During 1978-79, he was project director for a policy panel on the future of US-China relations sponsored by the United Nations Association of the United States of America. In mid-1979 he became executive director of The Yale-China Association.

Foreword

China has been a big story for as long as any of us can remember--and longer. Often, it has been a difficult and frustrating story for both the reporter and the public to understand.

For many if not most Americans, the China story has stirred the imagination from its beginnings almost two hundred years ago: a great confusion of images and ideas, of fact and fiction, of reality and fantasy that has produced exaggerated expectations and disappointments, an emotional involvement that at times has seemed an obsession, that has affected our domestic policies as much as our foreign policy, and that at all times has captivated our media.

However good our training or noble our intentions, it is unlikely that we travel to China with only a typewriter and a blank reporter's notebook. Rather we carry with us assumptions, instincts, and even labels that aren't easily applied to a culture, and to a political and social system that is outside our own experience and that of our audience. There persists the need to be a cultural mediator as well as a reporter.

Recent surveys tell us that most Americans learn most of what they know of foreign affairs from the media, broadcasting and print. If so, an informed public depends more than ever on an informed journalism.

It is in recognition of those needs, and of the crucial alliance of scholar and journalist in fulfilling them, that the China Council of The Asia Society has published the essays in this volume.

Irv Drasnin
New York City

Acknowledgements

Although our names grace the cover of this book, we readily acknowledge our debt to many individuals and organizations who made it possible. To them goes the credit of making China Briefing, 1981 what it is. We take responsibility for the errors that undoubtedly remain, but prefer to focus on the help we received from:
 --the authors, whose essays were originally distributed as background papers to American print and broadcast journalists.
 --many China Council members and associates who reviewed the essays prior to publication.
 --Jonathan Daen, the Council's former administrative assistant, whose help in preparing the typescript was invaluable.
 --other members of the staff of The Asia Society's China Council and Washington Center.
 --Martha Bush, who did much of the proofreading.
 --Irv Drasnin and Ezra Vogel, the Council's co-chairmen, who have provided consistently sound advice.
 --Phillips Talbot, retiring president of The Asia Society, who has vigorously encouraged the China Council effort.
 --The National Endowment for the Humanities, The Henry Luce Foundation, The Rockefeller Brothers Fund, and The Rockefeller Foundation, the Council's financial supporters.
 --The fine staff at Westview Press, led by Fred Praeger and Lynne Rienner.

> Robert B. Oxnam
> Richard C. Bush
>
> Washington, D.C.

A Note on Romanization

How to render Chinese words into written English has been the subject of a long debate. Politics and linguistic theory are both involved.

For many years, the Wade-Giles system, devised by two nineteenth century British diplomats, was the standard for all but names of prominent places. These were rendered in the Postal Atlas system (for example, Peking in the Postal Atlas system is Peiching in Wade-Giles). Both systems had their share of anomalies, and a number of alternatives were proposed over the years. One of these, called pinyin (literally "phonetic spelling"), was adopted by the People's Republic of China for limited internal use in the late 1950s. But in its publications distributed in the English-speaking world, the PRC retained a modified version of the Wade-Giles and Postal Atlas systems. That situation ended on January 1, 1979 when the PRC switched to pinyin for its foreign publications. Most American newspapers, newsmagazines, and journals followed suit.

This volume employs pinyin throughout (except for the familiar rendering of Chiang Kai-shek). Because many readers will be more familiar with the Wade-Giles forms, and because pinyin introduces some new anomalies, the next page provides a conversion table of proper names for which the current and previous systems differ.

Pinyin	Wade-Giles/Postal Atlas	Pinyin	Wade-Giles/Postal Atlas
Anhui	Anhwei	Ma Tianshui	Ma Tien-shui
Baoshan	Pao-shan	Mao Yuanxin	Mao Yuan-hsin
Beijing	Peking	Mao Zedong	Mao Tse-tung
Bo Yibo	Po Yi-po	Nanjing	Nanking
Bohai	Pohai	Ni Zhifu	Ni Chih-fu
Chai Zemin	Ch'ai Tse-min	Nie Rongzhen	Nieh Jung-chen
Chen Muhua	Ch'en Mu-hua	Peng Chong	P'eng Ch'ung
Chen Xilian	Ch'en Hsi-lien	Peng Zhen	P'eng Chen
Chen Yonggui	Ch'en Yung-kuei	Qinghua	Tsinghua
Chen Yun	Ch'en Yun	Shaanxi	Shensi
Chengdu	Chengtu	Shandong	Shantung
Chongqing	Chungking	Shanxi	Shansi
Daqing	Ta-ch'ing	Sichuan	Szechwan
Dazhai	Ta-chai	Song Renqiong	Sung Jen-ch'iung
Deng Xiaoping	Teng Hsiao-p'ing	Song Zhenmin	Sung Chen-min
Deng Yingchao	Teng Ying-ch'ao	Tiananmen	Tien-an-men
Fu Yuehua	Fu Yueh-hua	Ulanhu	Ulanfu
Fudan	Futan	Wang Dongxing	Wang Tung-hsing
Fujian	Fukien	Wang Hongwen	Wang Hung-wen
Fuzhou	Foochow	Wang Rongzhen	Wang Jung-chen
Geng Biao	Keng Piao	Wang Zhen	Wang Chen
Guangdong	Kwangtung	Wei Guoqing	Wei Kuo-ch'ing
Guangxi	Kwangsi	Wei Jingsheng	Wei Ching-sheng
Guangzhou	Kwangchow	Wu De	Wu Te
Hebei	Hopei	Xinjiang	Sinkiang
Henan	Honan	Xiyang	Hsi-yang
Hu Yaobang	Hu Yao-pang	Xu Shiyou	Hsu Shih-yu
Hua Guofeng	Hua Kuo-feng	Xu Xiangqian	Hsu Hsiang-ch'ien
Hubei	Hupeh	Yangzhou	Yangchow
Ji Dengkui	Chi Teng-k'ui	Yangzi	Yangtze
Jiang Qing	Chiang Ch'ing	Yang Yong	Yang Yung
Jiangsu	Kiangsu	Ye Jianying	Yeh Chien-ying
Jiangxi	Kiangsi	Yu Qiuli	Yu Ch'iu-li
Kang Shi'en	K'ang Shih-en	Zhang Aiping	Chang Ai-p'ing
Li Desheng	Li Te-sheng	Zhang Chunqiao	Chang Ch'un-ch'iao
Li Xiannian	Li Hsien-nien	Zhang Guangdou	Chang Kuang-tou
Lin Biao	Lin Piao	Zhang Tingfa	Chang T'ing-fa
Liu Bocheng	Liu Po-ch'eng	Zhao Ziyang	Chao Tzu-yang
Liu Shaoqi	Liu Shao-ch'i	Zhejiang	Chekiang
Liu Xinwu	Liu Hsin-wu	Zhou Enlai	Chou En-lai

Source: US Department of State, "Background Notes: China," March 1980. The dotted line denotes the July 1, 1979 expansion of Inner Mongolia (Nei Monggol), whereby the autonomous region received the western portions of Heilongjiang and Jilin provinces, and the northern portions of Liaoning and Gansu provinces and of the Ningxia Hui Autonomous Region. This change restored the borders existing before July 1969.

1
Introduction

Robert B. Oxnam

China Briefing 1981, like its predecessor China Briefing 1980, is an offshoot of the media activities of the China Council of The Asia Society. The Council began in the mid-1970s to provide American print and broadcast journalists with background information about current developments in China. As the pace of US interest in China accelerated in the late 1970s and early 1980s, this information network grew across the country and overseas as well. Soon, others beyond the journalist community--college students and professors, high school teachers, business executives, and China travelers--began requesting copies of the Council's briefing packets. To meet this demand, the Council and Westview Press last year embarked on a series of China Briefings, annual compilations of the Council's background essays. Both have been gratified by the widespread appeal and use of this type of publication.

China Briefing 1981 attempts a momentous task in a short space. It seeks to provide a readable overview of what is happening in a country of a billion people living halfway around the world. It endeavors to provide a quick, multifaceted portrait that covers not only politics, economics, and foreign policy, but also society, culture, and personalities. And it tries to convey the insights of American sinologists to broad audiences of nonspecialists who have become intrigued by China through commerce, study, travel, or whatever.

In short, we are trying to take China's pulse every year even though the patient is a long way off and our instruments much less precise than those of the medical profession. Rather than trying to say everything, we have emphasized brevity. What holds the book together are several themes that weave in and out of the chapters, each of which is authored by a different American China specialist. In these introductory comments, let us outline a few of these major unifying themes.

One theme concerns us <u>outsiders as much as it does</u>

the Chinese. Compared to five years ago, Americans have a much greater access to China. Today there are a number of American journalists resident in China, several hundred American students and scholars working in China, over a thousand American business people negotiating in China, and possibly a hundred thousand American tourists visiting China in 1981. In Beijing and a hundred other centers around the country, the Chinese are beginning to give access to schools and research institutes, libraries, factories and communes, residential areas, and archeological sites. Of course the process has not been easy and there are institutions, locations, and archives which have not been opened or only partially opened to foreign eyes.

But the trend line is clear and it is clearly reflected in the sense of immediacy and detail in the subsequent chapters. Thomas Gold of Harvard University, for instance, gives us remarkable insights into Chinese youth based on more than a year's residence in Shanghai and other cities. He reveals the widespread political alienation among younger people in China, and yet portays the differing pespectives of various generations of the more than five hundred million Chinese under thirty years of age. Drawing on extensive research and travel in the PRC, Deborah Davis-Friedmann of Yale University concentrates on Chinese family life. Her reflections, centering on the more than two hundred million family households in China, give us a mixed image. On the one hand, we discover the vitality and durability of the Chinese family system, contrasting sharply with the reports a couple of decades ago of its destruction. On the other hand, she also notes that the large size and close ties of family units may ultimately pose serious obstacles to the current effort for rapid modernization. Closely related to increased outside access is the growing Chinese candor about domestic problems. A few years back most outside observers were presented a rosy picture of Chinese accomplishments in the Cultural Revolution of the late 1960s and its aftermath in the early 1970s. Since the death of Mao Zedong in 1976, and even more so since the policy of economic readjustment in 1979, Chinese authorities and press have been much more forthright in pointing to serious political, social, and economic difficulties. We see this clearly in the chapter by Bruce Reynolds of Union College who cites the proliferation of Chinese reports about droughts, decline in grain output, serious budget deficits, rapid increases in inflation, growing unemployment, and decreased factory productivity. We also see this in the chapter by Richard Baum of UCLA, which recounts the enormous political dilemmas confronting China--bureaucratic obstructionism, nepotism and other forms of favoritism, election irregularities at the local level, and an aged ruling group at all levels. Once again, these conclusions are based primarily on Chinese reports. If the bloom is off the Chinese rose, it is as much the Chinese as the foreigners who have been plucking it away.

A second theme is China's apparent entry into a second phase of its recovery from the Maoist era and its plans for realizing the "four modernizations." The period of 1976-78 was characterized by widespread political euphoria after Mao's death, the purge of the most notable Cultural Revolution leaders and beneficiaries, the announcement of overly optimistic economic plans, and a general belief that the utopia of "comprehensive modernization" could be reached by the year 2000. The period of 1979-81 has been characterized by a more somber and realistic atmosphere, and many of the authors in this volume capture that mood. The new economic policies of the 1970s have undergone a more rigorous review and the 1980s economic catchwords are "readjustment" and "reform." Production targets have been scaled down considerably; light industry and agriculture now receive greater emphasis than heavy industry and energy; the consumer sector is increasingly in the economic limelight; recentralization and government planning have renewed attention; and foreign trade goals have been substantially curtailed.

The Chinese have also recognized the old adage that one cannot lead faster than the people are willing to be led. Policies announced at the top cannot be implemented in the provinces and at lower levels without restructuring and reforming the bureaucracy. For millenia, bureaucracy has been China's source of continuity as well as its source of frustration. The current leadership is confronting this enduring fact of political life in China and candidly revealing its frustrations.

One is reminded of the old Czech joke about the two stages of socialism: the first stage reveals the difficulties of development, and the second stage the development of difficulties. Nevertheless it is important to keep the current phase in somewhat broader perspective. China has indeed changed since the Maoist era and those changes are visible at many levels. Between 1977 and 1980 the new regime has achieved significant economic results. Grain production has increased by around 15 percent, and the output of cotton cloth has grown by 31 percent. The state has raised the prices at which it purchase agricultural goods on a compulsory basis by an average of 25 percent. Foreign trade has almost tripled. Similarly the educational establishment has been overhauled and the opportunities for advanced study have increased dramatically. Outside observers as well as Chinese note a much more open spirit in everyday life, one that is particularly evident among Chinese intellectuals and scientists.

So the current mood is one of cautious optimism interlaced with a certain amount of anxiety. Nowhere is this mood better revealed than in the areas of politics and ideology. As Richard Baum details, the premiere event of 1980 was the trial and conviction of the "gang of four" (including Mao Zedong's widow). It was a political purge, an attack on the Cultural Revolution, a policy reaffirmation for the new regime, and a television spectacular all wrapped up into one. At the same time, China's intrepid modernizer, Deng Xiaoping, heightened the attack on Mao's successor as chairman, Hua Guofeng, and placed close associates in key positions, most notably the new premier, Zhao Ziyang, and the Party's general secretary, Hu Yaobang. Richard Bush of The Asia Society's China Council offers us a portrait of Hu Yaobang and demonstrates how closely his career has followed that of his mentor Deng Xiaoping.

The third theme concerns <u>the many uncertainties facing Chinese politics</u>. The process of generational succession, even at the very top, has moved at a rather slow pace. Other than Hu Yaobang and Zhao Ziyang and a few others, little is known about the experience and competence of the successor generations, especially those who are taking over at the lower levels of the government and Party bureaucracy. A big unknown is what will happen after Deng Xiaoping's death. Deng, in spite of his seventy-seven years of age, has remained a dynamic integrating force in Chinese politics as he has sought to perpetuate his policies and promote his lieutenants. After his death, the leadership will probably seek a collective approach to governance, but that very approach has often foundered in the past as various leaders sought prominence for themselves and pushed different policies.

At an even deeper level, the post-Mao leadership has yet to find a new formula for its long-term legitimacy. The regime has gone a long way toward debunking the Mao of the Cultural Revolution and the Maoism which he fostered. Yet the final verdict on Mao has not been rendered and this coming year may yield new information on this matter. Here the new leadership finds itself caught between the victims of the Cultural Revolution, many of whom have now been restored to power, and the previous beneficiaries of the Cultural Revolution, like Red Guards who now find themselves frustrated outcasts.

While the post-Mao regime has gained considerable support in its selective de-Maoification and its modernization program, it has yet to develop the broad ideological consensus that provided unity and growth in China's past. While some have suggested that Chinese nationalism will form a basis for consensus, the present regime has yet to develop fresh and engaging bonds of national loyalty. Others have hoped that Chinese culturalism--or perhaps a fresh combination of traditional outlooks,

Chinese Marxism, and Western pragmatism--might be a new ideological sparkplug. Still others, including the present leadership, hope a revitalized, service-oriented Chinese Communist Party might provide political direction as well as ideological energy. But against these hopes, some of our authors point out countervailing trends--such as the growing privatism of youth and possibly the persistent familialism, albeit in socialist dress.

A final theme takes us away from China's domestic condition to China's international roles. In the post-Mao era, China has clearly taken a turn toward the outside world and that general trend continued strongly in the past year. In its economic and political relations, China continues to be an active force in world affairs and has continued its ties with Japan, other Asian countries, Western Europe, as well as the United States.

But, as with China's internal situation, some clouds have appeared on its international horizons. John Bryan Starr of The Yale-China Association points out that 1980 brought full normalization of legal and commercial relations between the US and China, but it also brought some post-normalization concerns. President Reagan's campaign comments about restoring official status to relations with Taiwan, as well as continued uncertainty about US arms sales to both Taiwan and the PRC, aroused anxieties in Beijing as well as elsewhere in Asia and the US. As Starr points out, however, the Reagan administration appears to have temporarily eased some of these concerns by endorsing the normalization communique while not, at least yet, making new overtures toward Taiwan. Another cloud has arisen over China's cutbacks in foreign trade which have been particularly sharp in terms of Sino-Japanese commercial relations. Indeed the whole matter of China's foreign commerce, although the overall amounts continue to grow, has caused some consternation among foreign businessmen who once had very high hopes for a large China market.

Thus, short, China Briefing 1981 tries to capture not only specific developments, but also the general mood emanating from China. It is not designed to be the last word on China, but rather to prod readers into exploring this fascinating, and often perplexing, country in greater depth. If it has that effect, then China Briefing 1981 will have achieved its purpose and we can test our speculations next year, when we turn our attention to China Briefing 1982.

Hu Yaobang (Eastfoto)

2
The Rise of Hu Yaobang and the Problems of One-Party Rule

Richard C. Bush

INTRODUCTION

Anyone making bets in September 1976, the month Mao Zedong died, on who would hold his post of Communist Party Chairman five years later probably did not put money on Hu Yaobang. Yet, on June 29, 1981 the Chinese Communist Party's Central Committee formally announced that Hu was Party chairman. out. As such, he will be a central figure in Chinese politics during the 1980s. Hu's rise is a mark of China's radical shift in direction since Mao's death, and of the lengths Deng Xiaoping has gone to insure a succession suited to his vision of the country's future.
Indeed, the heavy favorite in a fall 1976 sweepstakes probably would have been Mao's chosen successor-- the man Hu replaced--Hua Guofeng. Unlike Hu, whose yo-yo-like career has paralleled Deng's, Hua rose steadily through the ranks, working at the local, provincial and national level. Unlike Hu, who could be portrayed as having only one patron (Deng), Hua gained the favor of Mao, Zhou Enlai, and other senior leaders. He seemed the perfect centrist, capable of using the conflict between the victims and beneficiaries of the Cultural Revolution to his own advantage.
Despite his assets, Hua himself became a key symbol in the political battles of the last half-decade precisely because Mao bet on him. Since 1977 Deng Xiaoping and his associates have worked to isolate Hua by promoting changes in policy, removing Hua's allies, and attacking Mao and his Cultural Revolution. In late 1980 the chairmanship became an issue and Hua was forced to resign. Deng then nominated Hu Yaobang, who is at least Hua's equal in energy and mortality.
The tasks now before Hu are reviving China's political institutions and restoring public confidence in the Communist regime. There is some irony in this, for these were two of the problems that Mao tried to solve through

the Cultural Revolution, during which Hu was purged. Moreover, some observers wonder whether replacing Hua with Hu will facilitate or impede those tasks. Does the smell of revenge and cronyism hang so much over this latest conflict that it jeopardizes needed reforms? Part of the answer may lie in Hu Yaobang himself, his career, and his vision of the Party's role.

JOINING THE REVOLUTION

> In counties like . . . Liuyang . . . nearly all the peasants have combined in the peasant associations or come under their leadership. It was on the strength of their extensive organization that the peasants went into action and within four months brought about a great revolution in the countryside, a revolution without parallel in history.
>
> Mao Zedong, 1927

Most first-generation Communist leaders, like Mao Zedong, Zhou Enlai, and Deng Xiaoping, encountered the Chinese revolution only after they had left their native places. For second-generation leaders like Hu Yaobang, revolution swept through their home districts, picking them up in the process.

The year 1927 was one of upheaval in China, particularly in Hu Yaobang's home province of Hunan. Nationalist armies under Chiang Kai-shek challenged warlords for control of major cities and transportation arteries. At the local level, new social forces attacked the status quo. In Hunan there were a number of peasant uprisings, particularly in the river valleys that converged on the capital city of Changsha. Mao Zedong, a native of Hunan, toured the area in early 1927, and the report of what he saw would immortalize the rice-roots rebellion. "In a very short time, several hundred million peasants . . . will rise like a mighty storm, like a hurricane, a force so swift and violent that no power, however great, will be able to hold it back."

The Hunanese county with the highest tenancy rate and the third largest peasant association (reportedly 139,140 members) was Liuyang, where Hu Yaobang was born to poor peasants in 1915. Later in 1927, the Liuyang county seat was to be one target of an "Autumn Harvest Uprising" that the Communist Party organized to lift its sagging fortunes. Mao recruited volunteers from Liuyang to compose one of the several military units that were to support the rebellion. The uprising failed, and Mao moved east into the mountains that straddled the border between Hunan and neighboring Jiangxi. But Communist underground work continued in Liuyang, and a small soviet (guerrilla base area) soon emerged. (Liuyang was the native place of several other now-prominent CCP leaders: senior Politburo member Wang Zhen, Party organization department head Song Renqiong, and military leader Yang Yong.)

It is not surpising that these revolutionary currents swept up young Hu Yaobang, though precisely when is uncertain. There is no record of Hu or any of his relatives joining the peasant association, but there is unconfirmed mention that he participated in the Autumn Harvest Uprising, at the age of twelve. Hu's official biography does state that he left Liuyang in 1929 at the age of fourteen and made his way to Mao's Jiangxi Soviet. There he was assigned to do propaganda and organizational work among young people. After joining the Communist Youth League in 1930, he later rose to become secretary-general of its central committee, and was admitted into the Communist Party in 1933. One year later Chiang Kai-shek's troops forced the Communists to abandon the Jiangxi base area and begin the famous Long March. Hu headed the Youth League branch of a Red Army unit that made the trek, one of many young soldiers sometimes called "little red devils."

Hu's career took a new and significant turn after the decimated Communist forces found a haven in the northwest in the wake of the Long March. In 1937 war broke out between Japan and China, and the Red Army joined the Nationalists in a "united front" to resist the invaders. Initially Hu worked in the nerve center of a network of political commissars who handled logistics, recruitment, and propaganda in support of the war effort. It may have been in this capacity that he caught the eye of Deng Xiaoping, the chief political commissar of one of the Red Army's four principal units. In any event, Hu was named political commissar to one of the units under Deng's jurisdiction in 1941, and the two men "shared weal and woe" for the next forty years.

THE COMMISSAR TAKES OFFICE

> A proletarian Party must . . . get rid of the stale and take in the fresh, for only thus can it be full of vitality. Without eliminating waste matter and absorbing fresh blood the Party has no vigor.
>
> Mao Zedong, mid-1960s

After making revolution for two decades, Hu Yaobang, like the Chinese Communist Party itself, shifted gears in 1949 and began to build a new China. Leninist principles led the CCP to prefer centralized rule and deep penetration of Chinese society. As time went on, however, there was mounting evidence of popular disaffection with the regime, and Mao ultimately decided that the only solution was to destroy the political structure he had helped to build. Hu Yaobang was trapped in the rubble.

Following the defeat of the Japanese in 1945 and the Nationalists in 1949, the armies in which Deng and Hu served moved into occupied China's southwest, including Deng's home province of Sichuan. Hu Yaobang was assigned to direct Party and administrative affairs in the province's north region, which probably included Deng's hometown. Two factors probably eased his transition to civilian life: to make up for his lack of schooling as a child, he took advantage of the educational opportunities the Party offered; and his commissar duties taught him a host of administrative skills.

In 1952 political storms in Beijing resulted in the transfer of Deng and Hu to the center. Hu returned to his original field of work, taking charge of the Communist Youth League. Deng gradually became head of the Party bureaucracy, and thereby Hu's superior. Hu became a Central Committee member in 1956, at forty-one one of the youngest members of that ninety-seven-person body.

The Youth League was an important element of the Party structure. It had twenty million members in 1956 (about 11 percent of China's youth) and grew considerably in later years. Moreover, the League was the Party's principal recruiting ground for new members. For any young Chinese who wished to climb the ladder of success, the Youth League was one of the first rungs. A former colleague recently gave Hu high marks for having been "solicitous and enlightened about young people's study, work, health, cultural and recreational life, and love life."

Party Chairman Mao Zedong took an increasingly dim view of the creeping careerism he saw emerging in China. He felt that Party bureaucrats had become a "new class," devoted to serving their own interests and unconcerned about training "revolutionary successors" among the younger generation. In short, as Mao expressed it in the Marxist lexicon, China was in danger of "revisionism," of sliding back toward "capitalism." He tried to get officials to improve their "work style" and to create citizen bodies to monitor government performance, but his colleagues refused to go along. Frustrated, Mao launched the "Great Proletarian Cultural Revolution" in 1966, attacking the Party apparatus and the leaders who controlled it.

The Youth League was one of the Cultural Revolution's first battlegrounds, and Hu Yaobang was thus one of its first victims. In July 1966 Mao charged that "The . . . Youth League should stand on the side of the student [i.e. Red Guard] movement. But instead it stands on the side of suppression. . . ." Hu was branded a "capitalist-roader" along with his patron Deng Xiaoping, Mao's heir-apparent Liu Shaoqi, and many other Party officials. Red Guards reportedly shaved Hu's head and forced him to crawl out of his house on his hands and knees in public humiliation. In April 1967 he was stripped of his posts.

FROM EXILE TO CHAIRMAN-DESIGNATE

> The entire Party considers the Cultural Revolution . . . a great calamity. There was nothing correct during all those ten years [1966-1976]; there was no activity which could be described as positive. Everything was negative. The economy, culture, and education, as well as our ideological policy and Party organizations, received serious blows without exception.
>
> Hu Yaobang, 1980

Once purged, Hu Yaobang remained hopeful that Mao's supporters would weaken and the victims of the Cultural Revolution would return to power. He supposedly told his son, "Either I will be killed or the radicals [leading the Cultural Revolution] will not survive more than ten years." As it turned out, his estimate of ten years was remarkably accurate.

At the outset of his exile, Hu had to submit to the Maoist methods of "tempering and remolding" alleged capitalist-roaders like himself. Hu himself has provided the only information about that experience. He was forced to live for two and a half years in a stable and clean cattle, perhaps to reacquaint himself with the hard life of the Chinese masses. Probably around 1970, he was sent to one of the many May Seventh Reeducation Schools that were set up to rid former officials of ideological impurity. Two and a half years later, he was allowed to return to Beijing but had to share his already modest apartment with another family. Though he received a salary, he was given no work.

Hu's return to power depended on three developments, all of which occurred in the late 1960s and early 1970s:

--First, the radicals and their Red Guard supporters would have to bring China to the point of collapse. Only then would Mao turn to moderate elements to restore order. That point arrived as early as 1969.

--Second, Defense Minister Lin Biao, who had been named Mao's successor in return for his support for the Cultural Revolution, would have to overplay his political hand. Only then would Mao agree to reduce the military's deep involvement in Chinese life and to return purged civilian administrators to power. Lin did cross Mao in 1970-71, allegedly dying in a plane crash after bungling an assassination attempt against Mao.

--Third, Zhou Enlai, the hope of the moderates,

would have to feel sufficiently weak politically to turn to someone as tough as Deng Xiaoping to lead the fight against the remaining radicals. That came in 1972 when Zhou was diagnosed as having stomach cancer.

Thus Deng returned to the minefield of Chinese politics in April 1973. By all accounts, he refused to compromise with the radicals, believing that what China needed was science not slogans, technology not turmoil, competent administratation not cult of personality. He worked vigorously to fortify the moderate position against the day when Mao would die. He regained his Politburo seat in early 1974 and, with Zhou in the hospital, assumed day-to-day responsibility for government and Party affairs in early 1975. He brought back disgraced colleagues and drafted policies that suited his emphasis on economic modernization.

Not surprisingly, Deng turned to Hu Yaobang for help in digging his political trenches. Sometime in mid-1975, he selected Hu to head a team charged with reviving the science establishment, both a principal target of the Cultural Revolution and a key to Deng's broader modernization strategy. Hu and others in Deng's brain trust quickly prepared a major policy proposal.

Clearly, Deng's approach was a growing threat to the "socialist new born things" of the Cultural Revolution, particularly in the fields of science and education. The radical leadership, later dubbed the "gang of four," went on the offensive in late 1975 and branded Hu's proposal "a poisonous weed." Then in January 1976, with the death of Zhou Enlai, the radicals vigorously lobbied Mao to block Deng's plan to succeed tha late premier. The April 1976 demonstrations in Beijing's Tiananmen Square--in memory of Zhou and in support of Deng-- apparently gave Mao cause to purge Deng again. Once again, Deng's close associates, Hu Yaobang included, joined him in exile.

Having taken two steps forward and one step back on their return to power, Deng and Hu began again. Major obstacles were removed with Mao's death in September 1976 and the purge of the "gang of four" (including Mao's widow) a month later. But several key supporters of the Cultural Revolution--Wang Dongxing, for example--remained in the central leadership, and they sought to strike a compromise by accepting modernization as a major goal but preserving as much as possible of the Maoist legacy. They initially tried to block Deng's second rehabilitation but finally relented, and Deng resumed his posts in July 1977. Hu Yaobang was restored to the Central Committee a month later at the Eleventh Party Congress.

Again, Deng refused to work in harness with the Cultural Revolution survivors. A master tactician, Deng fought a series of political battles on multiple fronts. He did not win all his fights, nor did victories come as fast as he would have liked. At times he has had to retreat in the face of opposition. But in the past four years he has reduced Mao's legacy to a small fraction, and Hu Yaobang has played a central role in three key areas.

1. The first area was gaining control of the Party apparatus, where the beneficiaries of the Cultural Revolution held many important levers of power. Not long after his return, Hu was named head of the Party organization department, which fills key leadership positions and, in recent years, rehabilitated many persons unjustly persecuted during the Cultural Revolution. He took a step up the ladder in late 1978, becoming secretary-general of the Party, responsible for daily work at headquarters in Beijing and supervision of subordinate organizations. At the same time, he assumed a leading role in the new Discipline Inspection Commission and took over the propaganda department from an ally of Hua's whose Maoist sympathies were too pronounced. Hu turned over the organization department to Song Renqiong, a long-time associate of Deng's who, like Hu, hailed from Liuyang county in Hunan.

Hu's dominance of the Party organization became even more clear in February 1980. The Central Committee restored the Secretariat, which was abolished during the Cultural Revolution, as its principal executive agency. Hu Yaobang was named to head it, with the more prestigious title of general secretary, the same that Deng Xiaoping held at the beginning of the Cultural Revolution. Hu, not Chairman Hua, would be responsible for implementing Party policy and supervising the functional departments such as organization and propaganda.

2. A second issue in which Hu was deeply involved was the evaluation of Mao's legacy. The criticisms of Mao began in late 1977 shortly after Deng's rehabilitation. Because guardians of the late chairman's memory were still fairly powerful at the time, the attack was slow and subtle at first. Then, in 1978, dogmatic reliance on Mao's teaching came under attack, with Hu advocating the principle that "practice [as opposed to theory] is the sole criterion of truth," and Deng advocating the slogan, "seek truth from facts." Hu was subsequently responsible for preparing major statements evaluating Mao's rule. One of these, released in October 1979, repudiated Mao's analysis in the early 1960s that China was turning revisionist (a more detailed judgment is to be released soon). Hu expressed his own views on Mao in June 1980. He acknowledged Mao's contributions to the revolution but was candid about Mao's mistakes as well. According to Hu, Mao late in life developed ideas that brought disaster to the Chinese Party and people.

3. The third area in which Hu played a prominent role was leadership succession, specifically the position of

Hua Guofeng. Mao had picked Hua to be his successor as Party chairman, probably in the hope that Hua could mediate between left and right and so avoid a Dengist China. Indeed, Hua did have assets. That Mao had chosen him was important for some. Hua played a central role in the smashing of the "gang of four." And he was supported by some Party elders who wanted to avoid another bitter succession battle, by Maoist survivors who valued his fairly positive evaluation of the late chairman, and by some economic planners whose views he shared. But Hua also had liabilities, which Deng exploited to Hu Yaobang's benefit. Many of Deng's initiatives--shifts in policy, the purge of remnant leftists, the mounting criticism of Mao and the Cultural Revolution--served to isolate Hua. Hua's own leadership since 1976 came in for criticism as well. (See the next chapter, by Richard Baum, for a fuller discussion of Hua's liabilities.)

As Hua's position deteriorated, Hu's improved. In late 1978 Hua had to make an initial self-criticism; Hu was elevated to the Party Politburo. In February 1980, Hua, under pressure, declared his intention to give up his post of premier of the State Council; Hu entered the Politburo's standing committee and became Party general secretary, thus isolating Hua from the organization he ostensibly headed.

In late 1980 Hua's detractors went on the offensive again. After a series of meetings in November and December, the Politburo decided that Hua's various "mistakes" made him unfit to continue as Chairman. Hua, the most visible symbol of Mao's final effort to preserve China in his image, offered his resignation and also gave up the concurrent post of head of the Party's Military Commission. Reportedly, the Politburo asked Deng to assume both of Hua's posts. Deng considered the offer for two days, and then nominated Hu Yaobang as Party chairman on the grounds that he was younger and more vigorous. (Since Deng had no suitable nominee for the Military Commission post, he took it himself on a temporary basis.) Ratification of Hu's elevation came at the Central Committee's sixth plenary session, which met in late June 1981 (Hua was made a Party vice chairman).

LOOKING TO THE FUTURE

> What is the danger [facing] a party after it has assumed power? The danger is that it will degenerate if it works carelessly. After it has assumed power, the party cannot order the masses and must not become [like] the rulers and ruling class of the old society.
>
> Hu Yaobang, 1980

Both Deng Xiaoping and Hu Yaobang believe strongly that China needs, in Deng's words, a "united force with a high degree of awareness and discipline" to "gather together the strength of the whole people . . . to achieve tremendous accomplishments." By the time of Mao's death, however, two decades of political conflict had sapped the Communist Party of much of its organizational vitality and public prestige.

Ironically, Hu Yaobang's principal problem--a bloated bureaucracy concerned only with protecting its vested interests--is the very one that Mao Zedong tried to solve through the Cultural Revolution that Hu has criticized so sharply. Hu clearly believes that a new round of turmoil is not the way to reform the Party. But he is employing some of the same techniques that Mao tried without success in the early 1960s. It remains to be seen whether Hu can succeed where Mao failed.

Hu himself gave the best description available of the disease that infects that Party organization:

> In some localities the unhealthy workstyle is quite serious among the Party members. For example, some have refused to implement the Party's line, principles, and policies, or have feigned compliance . . . in public but opposed [them]. . . in private. Some have used the authority the people give them for private interests, to form their own factions and assign their own people to various posts. Some have . . . established illicit relations by giving banquets and gifts, practicing favoritism and accepting bribes, thus impairing the prestige of the Party and the state and squandering the property of the state and collectives. A small number of people have used their powers to frame and persecute good people. Some have practiced fraud, deceived their superiors and deluded their subordinates, resorted to boasting and flattery and acted opportunistically . . . . These unhealthy tendencies have impaired the Party's prestige, undermined the relationship between the Party and the people, weakened the Party's fighting capability and abetted . . . unhealthy [social] practices.

Some of the measures Hu has proposed to deal with these problems have a deja vu quality to them. The first of these is reeducation of officials, changing their behavior by changing their values. To this end, the Party's Discipline Inspection Commission issued in March 1980 twelve "guiding principles on inner-Party life." Second, local-level politics is to be democratized, creating popular checks on officialdom. And third, Hu and others have advocated far-reaching institutional changes to remove what are seen to be the structural causes of bureaucratism. Included in these reforms are collective leadership of Party committees at all levels (as opposed to one-man rule), mandatory retirement for older officials to facilitate an infusion of new blood, and opening up Party membership to individuals with expertise relevant to economic modernization (to reduce the influence of veteran members whose primary qualifications are political dexterity).

Though these are momentous tasks, there is no doubt about the energy and commitment Hu Yaobang will devote to them. He is described as being low-key and easy going, a good organizer and tough administrator, a powerful public speaker possessing the will of a "political gladiator." A former colleague now living in Hong Kong thought he had the right qualities to lead China during a period of change:

> Hu Yaobang's workstyle is realistic, following the principles of "seeking truth from facts." Because he was long engaged in youth work, he tends to be openminded and adapts to new things with relative ease. For modernization and democratization, this will be an advantage.

That same colleague, however, faulted Hu for what was termed a "blind faith in the strength of the Party," and that may become a serious obstacle. Mao Zedong tried the first two of these measures in different forms during the early 1960s, and they did not work. Whether it is ever possible to change the values of bureaucrats who have deep institutional and personal interests is questionable. How to prevent local-level officials from co-opting their new citizen guardians is uncertain. If the effectiveness of these measures, which operate at the margins of Party rule, is open to doubt, can the third part of the reform package--which strikes at the heart of the Communist structure--be adopted, much less successfully implemented?

Hu Yaobang has not given up on the possibliity of the Chinese Communist Party's correcting its many problems, even though the reform momentum seems to have slowed in early 1981. Nor has he given into those who say that the organization cannot accommodate to change or does not need it, though he may if his "faith" truly is "blind." The odds are that the Party, thirty-eight million members strong and half of those recruited during the Cultural Revolution decade, will get the better of him. But if Hu is the ultimate victor, he will have brought about an institutional revolution of major proportions.

3
From Feudal Patriarchy to Rule of Law: Chinese Politics in 1980

Richard Baum

As necessity is the mother of invention, so crisis is the mother of reform--with great crises typically begetting great reforms. The truth of this axiom was nowhere more vividly illustrated in 1980 than in the People's Republic of China (PRC). Emerging from more than ten years of chaos and destruction brought on by Mao Zedong's tumultuous Great Proletarian Cultural Revolution, beset by economic difficulties and the loss of public confidence in the Chinese Communist Party (CCP) and government leadership, the PRC entered the 1980s facing one of the most profound political crises of its thirty-year history.

So deep and so widespread were the bitter residues of alienation and demoralization stemming from China's decade of destruction that Beijing's leaders in 1980 openly acknowledged the near collapse of their political authority. Calling the need for reform a matter of "life or death" for China's socialist system, the CCP turned its back on the Maoist legacy--now indirectly characterized as a "feudal patriarchy"--and took the first tentative steps toward establishing a radically new institutional framework of "socialist democracy" and the "rule of law."

Reflecting the perceived seriousness of China's crisis of confidence, the new reforms were drastic indeed. They included, among other things, free elections at the grass-roots level; due process of law; the principle of ministerial accountability; separation of Party and state (with enhanced autonomy for the latter); and a merit system of cadre appointment, promotion, dismissal, and retirement.*

---

*Some of these reforms were first introduced experimentally in 1979. See David M. Lampton, "Politics in the PRC: Entering the Fourth Decade," in China Briefing, 1980.

At the same time, the new regime consciously abandoned or attenuated many of the CCP's oldest and most venerated shibboleths--including the myth of the infallibility of the Supreme Leader; the "Dazhai Spirit" of egalitarianism and self-reliance; the Maoist ethos of "politics in command"; and unbridled faith in the superiority of state planning over market regulation of the economy.

The very radicalism of these measures, many of which cut to the core of China's Communist system, proved difficult for some traditionalists to accept. In a society long dominated by orthodox Mao-thought and governed by deeply entrenched bureaucratic interests, it was inevitable that new conflicts would emerge. Consequently, many of the erstwhile Party faithful implemented the reforms only with profound misgivings and substantial hesitation.

Signs of political tension and uncertainty were manifold in 1980:

— The long-awaited trial of the "gang of four" was repeatedly postponed throughout the year, as was the full implementation of a widely heralded comprehensive code of criminal procedure, formally promulgated on January 1.

— The newly endorsed principle of freedom of political expression was partially vitiated by being made conditional upon the promotion of "stability and unity" and the upholding of Marxism-Leninism.

— The well-publicized inauguration of free, democratic elections at the local level was marred by widespread complaints of electoral fraud and manipulation, as local officials balked at the prospect of having to relinquish their traditional autocratic prerogatives.

— There was a major shakeup of the government leadership, as Premier Hua Guofeng and seven deputy premiers resigned in September, in some cases under duress. Allegations of corruption and malfeasance in high places multiplied throughout the year.

— New steps were taken to reduce Party control over management of the economy and to decentralize economic decision making, until mounting inflation forced a reimposition of some central controls.

The principal victim of this reform movement was the legacy of Mao Zedong. As the late chairman's successors grappled with the delicate problem of assigning primary responsibility for the "disastrous" Cultural Revolution, his role in modern Chinese history was alternately defended and derided. By the end of the year, virtually all that remained of the once canonical "Thought of Mao Zedong" was a classical admonition to "seek truth from facts." Mao's ghost hovered over the single most spectacular political event of 1980, the trial of the "gang of four," which began in November. Though not the object of a formal criminal judgment, the late chairman

could not escape being identified in the public mind as an unindicted coconspirator.
The second victim was Party Chairman Hua Guofeng, Mao's handpicked successor and the last remaining top-level cultural revolutionary holdover. China's pragmatic modernizers, led by the irrepressible septuagenarian Deng Xiaoping, forced Hua to resign the post of premier and drastically curtailed his authority within the Party. By year's end Hua was a marked man--vulnerable to charges of economic incompetence, political illegitimacy, and guilt by association in the misdeeds of the "gang of four." Even his incumbency as chairman was in doubt.
In all, it was a year of dramatic and painful reconstruction, as China's leaders sought to breathe new life--and credibility--into the country's outworn, ossified political institutions. Whether all the storm and fury would make a lasting difference was another question.

THE CRISIS OF FAITH

The sweeping political and institutional changes were initiated in response to widespread public disenchantment, first manifested in 1978-79 and openly admitted by Deng Xiaoping in a major policy address delivered in mid-January 1980. "At present," Deng stated, "some people, especially some young people, doubt the socialist system and babble that socialism is inferior to capitalism." Acknowledging that "serious shortcomings" existed in the economic and political work of the Party and government, Deng tied the realization of the four modernizations to the improvement of public confidence in socialism. "Without that," he warned, "all our boasting will be useless."
Signs of the popular malaise were everywhere. In an opinion poll conducted by China's Institute of Psychology, fully 89 percent of a sample of 343 workers in an unnamed factory stated that the local Party officials should either be popularly elected or chosen through "free competition," rather than appointed from above, as was customary. Asked to comment on the major sources of their own personal dissatisfaction, the workers' most frequent response was "bad leadership," followed closely by "low wages," "housing problems," "leader privileges," "dullness of life," "factionalism," and "poor education of children." In a remarkable display of apolitical candor that would have been unthinkable in the past, one young student interviewed by a Chinese journalist ventured the opinion that "Life should be rich, colorful, and full of pizzazz"--hardly the stuff of which revolutionary dreams are made.
The alienation of youth was a particular source of difficulty. The media candidly reported a dramatic

upsurge in juvenile gang-related activities, with armed robbery, burglary, rape, smuggling, gambling, and prostitution said to be reaching alarming proportions. Judicial authorities in the city of Wuhan processed more than 22,000 juvenile offenders in the twelve months from April 1979 to April 1980. The most extreme example of youthful alienation concerned a frustrated young veteran of China's "rustication" movement of the late 1960s. Reportedly despondent over the government's persistent refusal to permit him to work near his family home in Beijing, he detonated a powerful homemade bomb in the crowded Beijing Railway Station in late October, killing himself along with eight others, and injuring eighty-three. Although the incident was officially treated as an isolated case of "criminal counterrevolutionary sabotage," subsequent media commentaries pointed to a great many unresolved "problems affecting the people's livelihood" left over from the ten years of cultural revolutionary chaos.

Interestingly, the responsibility for such problems began to shift. From 1977 to 1979, virtually all such problems had been blamed on the "pernicious influence" of Lin Biao and the "gang of four." By 1980, however, this standard explanation had lost much of its public credibility. Increasingly, the Party itself was being held responsible for the manifold difficulties besetting Chinese society. The Party journal Red Flag openly acknowledged that "The Party's prestige is not high at present--this is a fact." And it was further stated that "Without improvement [the Party] cannot persist in leadership." Party General Secretary Hu Yaobang sounded a similar note at a Party conference held in late autumn of 1980. He suggested that the policy changes implemented since Mao's death in 1976 had been insufficient to correct the mistakes of the previous two decades, and termed further reform of Party leadership a matter of "life and death."

STRENGTHENING SOCIALIST DEMOCRACY

One problem that gave Hu special concern was the Party's tendency to monopolize powers more properly vested in representative assemblies and state administrative bodies. To curb this "autocratic tendency," and to prevent future abuses of power on the part of arrogant and irresponsible Party officials, a number of major institutional reforms were initiated in 1980, under the rubric of "strengthening socialist democracy and the rule of law."

One of the most prominent reforms--direct popular elections of delegates to county people's congresses--marked a significant change in the Chinese concept of popular representation. Previously, local elections had largely been routinized displays of rubber-stamp acclamation, controlled and manipulated by local elites. As one resident of Zhejiang Province put it, "What is an election but a list of candidates put up by the authorities for voters to endorse?"

The new procedures were designed to deal with such skepticism. Instead of voting on a short list of pre-screened candidates drawn up by Party and government officials, citizens were now encouraged to nominate freely their own candidates without threat of higher-level veto. By requiring the number of nominees to substantially exceed the number to be elected, and by introducing the secret ballot to prevent cadre intimidation of voters, the new system was designed to promote greater openness and meaningful choice in the electoral process. Indeed, several independent candidates outpolled their Party-backed opponents; and in a few isolated cases, avowed non-Marxists actually secured election.

Marring the new experiment in grass-roots democracy were frequent allegations of electoral manipulation and fraud, ostensibly perpetrated by local officials reluctant to relinquish their traditional privileges. The most widely publicized case occurred in Hunan Province, where local cadres reportedly sought to bar the election of a self-professed non-Marxist student. In protest over the cadres' heavy-handed tactics, eighty-seven of the student's classmates went on a three-day hunger strike, while 4,000 young people took to the streets of the provincial capital to demonstrate against the "undemocratic running of local elections."

Despite such hanky-panky, the experiment in electoral democracy was by and large successful. Tested in a few select areas in the first half of 1980, the new system was being implemented on a nationwide basis by year's end. Although some outside observers (as well as some Chinese participants) remained highly skeptical of the "showcase" nature of the electoral reforms, the new system carried with it profound implications for the reform of local politics, long dominated by the present-day equivalent of China's traditional "feudal gentry."

Paralleling the direct election of local people's congresses was the experimental adoption of democratic elections in many state-owned industrial enterprises. Two principal forms of industrial democracy were introduced in 1980: direct election of workshop cadres (replacing the traditional system of higher-level appointment); and direct election of factorywide workers' congresses, resurrected after more than twenty years. The dominant policymaking role of Party committees in industrial enterprises was severely reduced in favor of greater control by professional managers, and the workers' congresses were given nominally expanded powers of administrative oversight and supervision within the enterprise.

These measures were all undertaken as part of a major effort to increase the quality, responsiveness, and accountability of enterprise management, while at the same time raising the morale (and hence the labor productivity) of the work force. Combined with new economic incentives for workers and greater local autonomy and flexibility for enterprise managers, the reforms gave China's thirty million state-employed factory workers their first real taste of industrial democracy since the mid-1950s.

Another major step toward "strengthening socialist democracy" was the government's adoption of the principle of ministerial accountability. At the third session of the Fifth National People's Congress (NPC), held in early September, delegates were given the unprecedented opportunity of querying government leaders at great length and in critical detail on a variety of controversial issues. At one session, a group of delegates from Beijing summoned the minister and two deputy ministers of the metallurgical industry to answer a series of pointed questions about an expensive, problem-ridden iron and steel complex being built at Baoshan, near Shanghai. During the course of the questioning it was revealed that the Baoshan complex had been poorly planned, badly sited, underfinanced, and inefficiently managed. Partially as a result of the publicity generated by this exposure, the entire Baoshan project was suspended pending governmental investigation. (Some observers feel that this ostensible display of government candor was actually a carefully calculated slap at Premier Hua Guofeng, who had personally approved the construction of the Baoshan complex in 1978.)

Other groups of NPC delegates queried officials over the government's inept and deceitful handling of the Bohai Gulf oil rig disaster of November 1979, which resulted in the loss of seventy-two lives. Public exposure and criticism of the Bohai coverup at the NPC culminated in the official censure of Vice Premier Kang Shi'en, the dismissal of the minister of petroleum, Song Zhenmin, and the filing of criminal charges of negligence against four other petroleum ministry officials. Still other NPC delegate groups raised sharp questions about inflation of commodity prices, unreasonable wage raises, environmental pollution, population growth, and bureaucratic inefficiency.

By thus allowing the NPC to play more than its traditional role as a ritualistic rubber-stamp body, the regime sought to convince a skeptical public, grown weary of empty slogans and unkept promises, that this time socialist democracy was for real. If this was indeed the objective, it apparently succeeded. For as one NPC delegate remarked, "I found myself pleased by the candidness of the government leaders, who lived up to the commitments to the people by not making false, pompous, meaningless reports pretending that everything was all right and nothing wrong. Haven't we had enough of that in the past?"

FEUDALISM, BUREAUCRATISM, AND THE RULE OF LAW

Just as democratic reform was designed to restore public faith in government, the rule of law was seen as the key to improving government performance across the board. Speaking at the NPC in September, Premier Hua Guofeng stated that "the genuine rule of law" was essential for both "consolidating and enhancing the stability and unity of our country" and "ensuring the smooth progress of modernization." Toward this end, a number of new legal statutes were enacted in 1980, including a criminal code, code of criminal procedure, marriage law, income tax law, law on joint ventures, and nationality law.
The trend toward codification of law, begun in 1979, was part of the regime's attempt to overcome the deeply entrenched traditions of "feudal patriarchy" (one-man rule) and "bureaucratism." These two evils, part of China's premodern cultural heritage, were now held largely responsible for the inadequacy of governmental performance over the previous thirty years.
The attack began in late 1979 with pointed warnings to Party and government cadres that the widespread practice of officials' abusing the authority of their positions to promote personal interests would no longer be tolerated. On New Year's Day, People's Daily bluntly asserted that "Everyone is equal before the law, and nobody is allowed privileges beyond the law." On January 16 Deng Xiaoping called for the abolition of special privileges for cadres, labeling this a "severe struggle" which would be carried out "at all levels and in all departments."
The regime's indictment against "poisonous vestiges of feudalism" was subsequently spelled out in the mass media. One discussion, published in June, noted that:

> Some comrades . . . lord it over their own organizations and the masses. Arbitrary as they are . . . they allow no one to say a word against their decisions . . . and they even retaliate against those who dare to criticize or answer back. . . . The prevalence of special privileges is a salient feature of bureaucratism. . . . Thirty years ago we completely smashed the state apparatus of the landlord class and the big bourgeoisie. . . . But the hankering for feudal prerogatives . . . has not been

> fully wiped out. . . . A few cadres still go after special privileges in daily life, much in the same way as in feudal society, where, when one man becomes an official, all the members of his family are respected as nobles, his wife is honored with a title, his children succeed to his title, and his relatives and friends also receive favors.

By the summer of 1980 it was openly acknowledged that China's feudal-style bureaucratic practices were "far worse than any other kind of bureaucratism in the world"-- a stern self-criticism indeed!

Demonstrating the seriousness with which the Party and government viewed the issue of combatting feudalism and bureaucratism in 1980, the media exposed numerous cases of official corruption and malfeasance in high places. One prominent case involved the minister of commerce, Wang Lei, who was accused of having lavishly entertained colleagues and clients on numerous occasions at a fashionable Beijing restaurant, repeatedly refusing to pay his bills on the grounds that the banquets had constituted a "public service." As a result of the public outcry generated by the exposure of this case, Minister Wang was publicly censured and required to pay his delinquent bills. This was only one of many negative examples of the regime's commitment to the principle of "universal equality before the law."

Deng Xiaoping and his colleagues went beyond such individual exposes to what they regarded as the source of feudalism and bureaucratic corruption: official personnel systems, particularly the absence of mandatory retirement. Since most leadership posts carried implicit lifetime tenure, China's Party, state, and military bureaucracies had come to be dominated by gerontocrats, many showing definite signs of mental or physical infirmity. One remarkably candid report noted:

> The personnel in leading posts at all levels generally tend to be senile. Many high-ranking leading comrades even tend to have difficulty in walking. . . . They cannot work with the same vim and vigor as when they were young.

Without a retirement system for leading cadres, it was predicted, "a new round of aging cadres will arise after a few years . . . and this will become a cyclical problem."

Because life tenure (the "iron rice bowl") placed a greater premium on seniority and political loyalty than on technical or administrative competence, it led to other problems. It promoted bureaucratic ossification, factionalism, and the formation of mutually protective alliances at all levels of the hierarchy. It also

stifled organizational innovation and blocked the upward mobility of technically more proficient younger cadres.
To deal with this situation, the Party Central Committee in February 1980 called for the introduction of a rigorous merit system of hiring, examining, promoting, and dismissing cadres. In addition, a new policy was introduced calling for the mandatory retirement of superannuated leading cadres. Such a system, it was argued, would facilitate the opening of careers to talent while increasing the efficiency and responsiveness of the bureaucracy by "cracking the iron rice bowl."
In a specific attack on one remnant of "feudal patriarchy," new guidelines were proposed in 1980 fixing the term of top-level Party and government leaders (including ministers of state, Central Committee members, NPC Standing Committee members, and so forth) at five years, with a maximum tenure of three consecutive terms, or fifteen years. By routinizing the process of political succession the twin principles of fixed terms and limited tenure would prevent the rise of a self-perpetuating patriarchy while reducing the likelihood of divisive top-level power struggles (and consequent purges).

RETIRING THE OLD GUARD, SEPARATING PARTY AND STATE

The first serious test of the regime's new policies concerning political retirement and succession occurred in September, at the National People's Congress. In an unprecedented move, senior Deputy Premier Deng Xiaoping-- principal architect of the new personnel policies-- retired from active government duties, taking with him six other elderly vice premiers, five vice chairmen of the NPC Standing Committee and, more significantly (albeit not unexpectedly), Premier Hua Guofeng himself.
In addition to Hua (sixty), and Deng (seventy-six), other retiring vice premiers included Li Xiannian (seventy-five), Chen Yun (eighty), Xu Xiangqian (seventy-eight), Wang Zhen (seventy-one), Wang Renzhong (seventy-three), and Chen Yonggui (sixty-seven). Retiring vice chairmen of the Standing Committee of the National People's Congress were Nie Rongzhen (eighty-one), and Liu Bocheng (eighty-eight), among others. Indeed, of all the veteran Chinese "elder statesmen" still active in 1980, only NPC Chairman Ye Jianying (eighty-two) remained in office.
The retirements were not without a political design. Deng himself was the chief beneficiary of this carefully orchestrated shakeup, which was in fact a superbly finessed chess gambit designed to reduce the power of Hua, Mao's chosen successor. Moreover, Deng had also personally selected and groomed Hua's successor as premier, sixty-one-year-old Zhao Ziyang. A veteran

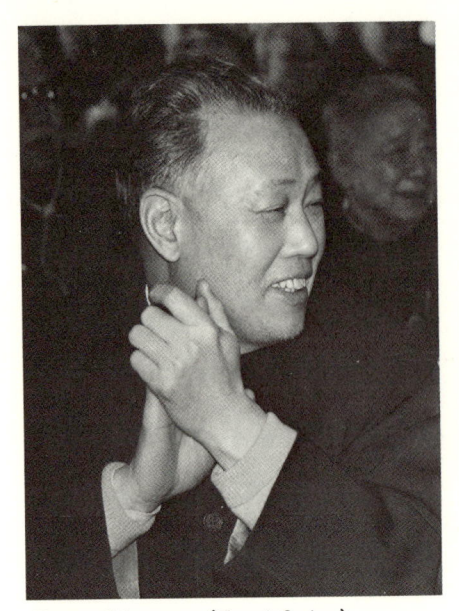

Zhao Ziyang (Eastfoto) 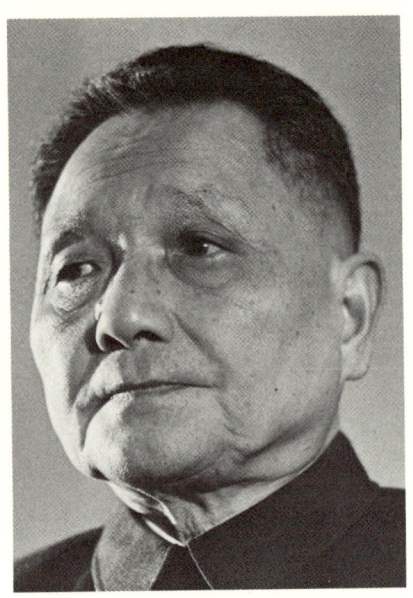   Deng Xiaoping (Sygma)

cadre, who like Deng had been purged as a "capitalist roader" during the Cultural Revolution, Zhao had been rehabilitated in the mid-1970s and placed in charge of the Party committee in populous Sichuan Province. In this post Zhao had personally underwritten a series of major socioeconomic and administrative reforms, including enhanced decision-making autonomy for industrial enterprises, free-market regulation of commodity production and distribution, heightened profit incentives for peasants, and a radical program of incentive-based birth control and family planning. Because of his personal sponsorship of these controversial reforms, Zhao's selection as premier was widely regarded as a victory for Deng's "pragmatic" faction.

Political maneuvering aside, the passing of the mantle of government leadership to Zhao and a new generation of technocratic "experts" did reflect a conscious policy decision to separate state administrative responsibility from Party authority. Thus none of the top government officials who resigned at the NPC simultaneously relinquished their leadership posts in the CCP.

The drive to separate Party leadership from state administration was ostensibly designed to overcome "overconcentration of power in the hands of a few individuals." By discouraging the widespread practice of individual leaders wearing "multiple hats" in various organizations, the new policy was also explicitly intended to aid in the promotion of younger cadres to positions of administrative responsibility--this despite the fact that the average age of the three new deputy premiers appointed at the NPC was fully sixty-six years.

MILITARY DISCONTENT

Hard hit by the regime's new personnel policies were China's senior military commanders. Seven were transferred to new regional posts, at least two were stripped of their concurrent top-level Party or government posts. Throughout the year there were frequent references in the media to the need for elderly, infirm senior officers to step aside in favor of "new blood." Not surprisingly, such suggestions apparently did not sit well with the army's high command.

There were mounting indications of incipient military unrest for other reasons. On the one hand, national defense had been assigned lowest priority among the four modernizations. In concrete terms, this meant that major new investments in up-to-date military hardware (including purchase of much-desired Western defense technology) would have to await the prior modernization of agriculture, industry, and science and technology. Among the rank-and-file of the People's Liberation Army-- long considered a loyal bastion of Mao-thought--<u>morale was ebbing because of agricultural policies that effectively discriminated against soldiers' relatives, mainly peasants</u>. The government responded with a program of "preferential treatment" for military dependents in the countryside, and by picking a professional officer, Deputy Chief of Staff Zhang Aiping, to be one of three new deputy premiers.

Despite such cosmetic concessions, the problem of flagging morale was further aggravated by political maneuvering. Outgoing Premier Hua Guofeng apparently sought to turn the latent discontent with the pragmatic policies of the Deng-Zhao regime to his own advantage. Resurrecting a long-buried slogan of the now discredited Cultural Revolution, Hua urged the military to "hold high" the Maoist banner of treating ideology as the "soul and commander" of all economic work. His gambit did not save him from being dumped as premier, but it did serve to further polarize the army. <u>At year's end, the highly publicized trial of five former high-ranking military officers, charged with involvement in a 1971 assassination attempt on Chairman Mao, further divided the military's political loyalties</u>.

All such conflicts paled in importance, however, before the most potentially divisive issue of them all: de-Maoization.

THE EXORCISM

Lurking ubiquitously in the shadows of Chinese politics in 1980, affecting everything it touched (and touching everything), lay the unquiet ghost of Mao Zedong. The Cultural Revolution now being renounced was Mao's own Cultural Revolution. The system of patriarchal power and privilege now undergoing reform in the name of "universal equality before the law" was, in essence, Mao's own system; the excesses of bureaucratic corruption and incompetence now under attack had been spawned under that system.

The posthumous reassessment of Mao's role in modern Chinese history began on a gentle, low-key note in 1978-79. Typical of this early phase was the publication in December 1979 of a set of "Study Notes on Mao Zedong Thought," written on the occasion of Mao's eighty-sixth birthday. Pointing out that Mao himself "for a long time did not agree to proposals for propagating Mao Zedong Thought," the study notes portrayed the late chairman as a modest (if not self-effacing) leader who opposed the extreme cult of personality that arose in the late 1960s. Stressing that Mao himself was "very much disgusted" by the actions of those who "out of ulterior motives tried to deify him," the study notes warned against the tendency to attribute all victories and all wisdom to the "genius" of any one man.

This initial effort at demythologizing Mao was followed shortly by publication of several articles criticizing the prevalent practice of using Maoist quotations to legitimize particular ideas, policies, or points of view. A People's Daily article in early January asserted that the mere "memorization of several quotations" was an "obsession" that had interfered with the scientific pursuit of knowledge. To prevent such a quotational obsession from recurring, the media obsessively quoted Mao's now-famous exhortation, "Seek truth from facts."

The next round came in early 1980, when Mao's successors attacked some of his pet theories and most controversial actions. People's Daily published an editorial that explicitly criticized Mao's famous theory concerning a continuing "two-line struggle" between the forces of socialism and those of capitalism. Mao asserted that this struggle was never ending, continuing even after a Communist Party came to power, and even affecting the Party itself. People's Daily now called the theory, which provided the major ideological justification for the Cultural Revolution, "distorted" and claimed that such struggles had actually occurred in "only a few cases" in the history of the Party.

Taking the argument one step further, the editorial called for a "correct appraisal" of cases that had previously been treated as instances of two-line struggle. High on the list was Liu Shaoqi, who was purged at Mao's personal behest as a "capitalist roader" during the Cultural Revolution (Liu died in disgrace in 1969). People's Daily labeled as "groundless" many of the Maoist allegations against Liu, noting that "Mao Zedong was a man, not a demi-god; he couldn't always be right and free from mistakes." As a result, Liu was posthumously rehabilitated and returned to favor at a Party Central Committee meeting in February 1980.

The mounting critique of Mao entered a qualitatively new stage in June. Party General Secretary Hu Yaobang bluntly derided some of Mao's economic theories as "not acceptable under new historical conditions" and claimed that Mao's errors during the Great Leap Forward (1958-60) and Cultural Revolution (1966-76) had "been the cause of great misfortune for the Party and the Chinese people." Calling the Cultural Revolution a total disaster, Hu stressed that Mao's theoretical mistakes had been "especially serious" during the last years of his life, when he was ill and thus "lacked energy"; consequently, Hu claimed, some of Mao's theories were not "rich in content" and were filled with "empty talk." Finally, Hu acknowledged what had hitherto been only implicit in the regime's mounting campaign against feudal remnants in the Chinese political system: that under Mao's tutelage China had been "a feudal monarchist state essentially for thirty years."

Suddenly in late summer, as Mao's portraits were removed from many prominent public locations in and around Beijing, the overt criticism declined noticeably. In part, this sudden lull reflected a tactical decision by Party and government leaders to delay a direct confrontation over Mao's historical legacy until after the September NPC and subsequent trial of the "gang of four." But it may also have been the result of a tacit deal between Deng and Hua to head off an open power struggle at the highest levels of Party leadership. <u>In return for Hua's resignation from the premiership, Deng would mute the campaign against Mao.</u>

While concern for preserving the appearance of intra-Party unity may have brought a temporary halt in the de-Maoization movement, Deng did not spare several of the late chairman's handpicked "model cadres" and "model units" from being exposed as frauds. Foremost among the Maoist standard bearers to be debunked in 1980 was the famous Dazhai production brigade in Shanxi Province, which had received Mao's blessing in the early 1960s as a nationwide exemplar of the spirit of self-reliance in agricultural development. Arguing that it had been wrong to "deify" Dazhai in the first place, the media alleged that there had been serious irregularities in Dazhai's self-reported production statistics over a period of several years. Primary blame for this deceit was assigned to the former Party secretary of the brigade, Chen Yonggui, who had risen during the Cultural Revolution under Mao's patronage to become deputy premier of the State Council and member of the Party Politburo. Following the exposure of his alleged misdeeds, Chen was stripped of his vice premiership at the September NPC.

Another calculated, if perhaps more subtle, slap at the legacy of Mao Zedong was criticism of the famous Maoist parable of "the foolish old man who moved the mountain." This allegorical morality tale, popularized during the Cultural Revolution, trumpeted the virtues and rewards of hard work, patience, and self-reliance. In 1980 it was ridiculed on the grounds that it "praised the foolish old man without taking into account his imbecility," while neglecting to expose the "utter impracticality of his approach." Indeed, the tone of this criticism strongly suggested that the "foolish old man" in question was not the erstwhile hero of the original fable, but rather Mao Zedong himself.

THE CASE AGAINST HUA

Nor was such sniping confined to oblique criticism of Chairman Mao. Early in the year, the first clear signs of an impending critique of Hua Guofeng were also detected. The February meeting of the Central Committee purged from the Politburo three of the principal actors in the infamous "Tiananmen Incident," the massive, spontaneous public demonstration of grief for the late Premier Zhou Enlai held in the nation's capital in early April 1976. The three--Beijing Military Region Commander Chen Xilian, Beijing Mayor Wu De, and commander of Beijing's elite "palace guard" (and Mao's personal bodyguard) Wang Dongxing--were loyal Maoists who had collaborated with the "gang of four" in forcibly suppressing the incident. Though the heavy-handed breakup of this demonstration had been condemned by the Party in 1978, the February dismissal of three of the top leaders judged responsible was widely interpreted as an act of public restitution. Another Maoist, Ji Dengkui, was dismissed from the Politburo at the same time, but was not linked directly with the Tiananmen Incident.

More significant than the disciplinary action taken against the four high-ranking Maoists--now collectively known as the "little gang of four"--was the action not taken against the one remaining top-level participant in the Tiananmen Incident. For in his (then) concurrent capacity as acting premier and minister of public security, Hua Guofeng had personally approved the use of public security units to help break up the April 1976 demonstration. The significance of this fact was not lost on certain segments of the Chinese population, some of whom

as early as December 1978 took to writing surreptitious wall posters demanding an investigation of Hua's role in the Tiananmen affair.
 Hua was exposed to public criticism for the first time in the summer of 1980, one month before the NPC. In an allegorical but nonetheless transparent article published in early August, Hua was implicitly likened to the "emperor's eunuch" in China's ancient Eastern Han dynasty, an opportunistic "puppet" who had achieved power following the emperor's death by conspiring with other court eunuchs to suppress a rival faction headed by "relatives of the empress."

Following Hua's resignation at the NPC, the pace of the incipient "de-Huaization" campaign quickened. Questioning the "autocratic" method by which Mao had personally selected Hua to succeed him as Party chairman, People's Daily argued in late September that a system under which "only the emperor has the right to name his successor" was a remnant of China's feudal past. Such a system was said to be "extremely dangerous" insofar as it "puts the political destiny of a country in the hands of one man alone." The power of a leader, the commentary continued, "is bestowed by the people"; therefore the leader "has no right to appoint his successor." A two-edged sword, this critique clearly impugned the legitimacy of both Mao (the appointer) and Hua (the appointee).

A tapestry commemorating the occasion on which Mao Zedong is said to have told Hua Guofeng, "With you in charge, I am at ease." (Picture by Terry Lautz)

Indeed, Hua was particularly vulnerable to such criticism. For his entire claim to succeed Mao as chairman rested exclusively on Mao's famous 1976 deathbed statement, "With you in charge, I am at ease." Although the Great Helmsman may have been at ease, there were obviously others--powerful others--who were not.

The campaign against Hua took another step forward with the publication in early autumn of an article which suggested that Hua, in his role as Party chairman, had condoned an official abuse of power. It was reported that a radio repairman in Xiyang county, Shanxi Province (location of the recently debunked Dazhai brigade), had been persecuted for having dared to expose the misdeeds of local officials. The article claimed that the repairman had written at least nine letters to Hua from 1976 to 1978, urging him to investigate the "abnormal" situation in Xiyang county. Hua failed to respond, and the repairman was allegedly sentenced to eighteen years in jail and beaten so badly that he became paralyzed.

By far the sharpest attack on Hua's leadership qualities came in early December, when he was tacitly but unmistakably held up to ridicule in the public media for having styled himself a "wise leader" who was entitled to "issue instructions" at will. His leadership style was termed "neither democratic nor scientific," and his economic policies (such as the decision to build the massive, ill-fated Baoshan iron and steel complex) were derided as "disastrous."

By year's end Hua was thus clearly on the defensive; and it was widely anticipated that he would be removed from the Party chairmanship at a Central Committee meeting scheduled to be held in spring 1981. Presumably, Hua would be replaced by Hu Yaobang, who in November 1980 had reportedly been promised an imminent "big promotion" by Deng Xiaoping.

THE LIMITS OF INDIVIDUAL FREEDOM

For all their efforts in 1980 to attack a repressive past and open up the political system, Deng and his associates still had to confront the potentially explosive issue of defining the tolerable limits of free expression and political dissent. The contradiction between democracy and discipline, between individual freedom and the need for national "stability and unity," was a permanent fact of life.

As the year began, the regime took a fairly hard line. In the wake of the late 1979 closure of Beijing's controversial "Democracy Wall" and the related trial and conviction of two prominent dissidents, Wei Jingsheng and Fu Yuehua, in late 1979, a major propaganda campaign against "extreme individualism" was launched. Taking as its main theme the idea that "it is impermissible to place democracy above the four modernizations," the new campaign stressed that extreme individualism was a feature of "bourgeois democracy" which "runs counter to the interests of the people." A newspaper commentary published in early January called extreme individualism a "new form of anarchism" and warned that "it is a kind of corruption [which] saps the morale of the people and sabotages stability and unity."

In a similar vein, Beijing in January released the text of an October 1979 interview by Deng Xiaoping. In that interview, Deng alleged that "There has appeared in our society a tendency towards anarchism and extreme individualism. . . . What we mean by extreme individualism is that the person in question wants absolute freedom for himself at the expense of . . . the freedom of others [and] the interests of the state." Calling such things "impermissible," Deng went on to state that Chinese citizens were "of course" free to express their opinions, but were "not allowed to attack and slander other people at will." Deng also alleged that under the pretext of promoting democracy, "a considerable number of people" had attempted to "stir up trouble," even going so far as to "ask the president of a foreign country to intervene in the so-called human rights [movement] in China." Calling such behavior "unreasonable," the deputy premier concluded that it was unnecessary "to warn these people that they too must abide by the laws."

Having thus laid down the human rights gauntlet, Deng proceeded to announce in mid-January <u>the imminent demise of the so-called "four big freedoms" which had been written into the Chinese constitution</u> after the Cultural Revolution, namely the <u>right to speak out freely</u>, <u>air views freely</u>, <u>hold big debates</u>, and <u>write big-character posters</u>. Arguing that such freedoms were "obviously inappropriate" insofar as they served to "encourage turmoil and hamper the four modernizations, democracy, and the legal system," Deng announced that China's constitution would be revised to abolish the "four bigs."

In an ironic underscoring of the regime's new priorities, with the four modernizations, and unity and stability taking precedence over "so-called human rights," Beijing's Democracy Wall was papered over with commercial advertisements in 1980. The "four bigs" were duly abolished by the NPC in September. And a partial crackdown on political dissidents began with the arrest of the editors of four small underground journals in early September.

In a related development, China's official policy of "letting one hundred flowers blossom" in the literary and artistic fields was dampened considerably in 1980 with the enunciation of <u>a series of explicit political criteria governing cultural expression</u>. In January Deng

Xiaoping reaffirmed the Party's traditional stance that "literature and art cannot be divorced from politics." In April a growing trend among contemporary writers to depict moods of public cynicism and despair in their literary works was decried in the mass media on the grounds that literature should "not only inspire people" but also "help people strengthen their confidence in Marxism-Leninism-Mao Zedong Thought."

An even more ominous critique of the recent literary trend toward depicting the "abnormalities and ugliness of society" was published in April in the form of an historical commentary on pre-World War I Russian literature. In 1913 Maxim Gorky had sought to suppress publication of the works of Feodor Dostoevsky on the grounds that by depicting the "spiritual emptiness" of Russian society, Dostoevsky "poured putrid poison on already benumbed souls, . . . helping the drowsy social conscience to sleep more soundly." Roundly endorsing Gorky's position in support of the principle of prior censorship, the commentary argued that writers should not lose sight of their "solemn obligations" to the societies they serve. Again quoting Gorky, the commentary ended with a sanctimonious flourish. "Photographing depressive spasms may be useful to medical science," it lectured, "but such things have nothing to do with art."

Publication of this dour commentary was followed in May by a call for the adoption of "new regulations on the content and style of articles." Arguing that "we must stress maintaining the leading position of Marxism and upholding Marxist superiority," a conference of literary and art workers in Hebei Province admonished all writers to study Marxism-Leninism-Mao Zedong Thought in order to "improve their ability to analyze life."

Signs of mounting political censorship increased noticeably in the latter half of the year. A writer in one province reportedly had his grain ration cut off following publication of an article highly critical of government bureaucracy. A popular television drama was banned in Shanghai for having cast the army in a less than heroic light. Several new plays were cancelled and their authors and actors harassed for having dared to deal with "politically provocative" themes. And in the educational system, teachers at several major Chinese universities were reportedly warned against the introduction of "unapproved materials" into classroom curricula.

The regime's concern for checking the "corrosive influence" of "decadent bourgeois ideas" had a more humorous side, at least to outsiders. In one incident, a provincial newspaper printed an attack on the "depiction of love stories in some movies and dramas." Noting that the recent introduction of foreign cultural influences had led to an upsurge of public interest in expressions of romantic love, the newspaper criticized the cinematic portrayal of young lovers "rolling on the grass, swimming romantically, and hugging and kissing." Such scenes reflected an "unhealthy trend," in the view of the author. In a related development, the military in mid-year launched a propaganda campaign among the ranks of its enlisted men designed to put an end to the "decadent practice" of adding off-color lyrics to traditional revolutionary songs.

And finally, following the official unveiling of a mural covering one full wall of a foreigners' restaurant inside Beijing's international airport, a scene depicting two bare-breasted minority nationality women was discreetly altered through the strategic interposition of a well-placed coatrack. Plus ca change. . . .

THE "GANG" STANDS TRIAL

Of all the momentous political dramas played out in China in 1980, none rivaled the long-awaited trial of the "gang of four" and the "Lin Biao clique" for sheer sensationalism and melodrama. Originally scheduled for mid-September, the trial was delayed more than two months as government prosecutors sought--in vain--to extract a prior confession of guilt from the gang's recalcitrant ringleader, Mao's widow, the sixty-seven-year-old Jiang Qing.

Along with Jiang and her three alleged "ultraleftist" coconspirators--former Politburo Standing Committee member Zhang Chunqiao, sixty-seven, former Party Vice Chairman Wang Hongwen, forty-five, and former Politburo member Yao Wenyuan, forty-nine--six other defendants, five of them military officers, faced trial on separate charges stemming from an unsuccessful 1971 attempt to assassinate Mao and stage a coup d'etat.

The case against the ten defendants was painstakingly prepared throughout 1980. Several hundred government investigators were dispatched to collect and sift through mountainous masses of evidential information. Twenty-four special prosecutors were assigned to argue the government's case in a special court presided over by no less than thirty-five judges. When the formal indictment against the defendants was finally handed down in mid-November, it ran to some twenty thousand words.

Insofar as the trial of the "Beijing Ten" provided the first significant test of the regime's new commitment to uphold the rule of law, strict observance of legal norms--in particular "due process"--was deemed vital in the government's handling of the case. Nevertheless, there were several legal ironies in the trial of the "gang." For one thing, a section of China's newly enacted code of criminal procedure, governing the maximum length of time accused criminals could be held without trial, was altered by special governmental decree in February 1980. This had the effect of exempting the "gang" from a key provision of the new code. For another thing, the defendants had been publicly declared guilty by Party and government leaders, and by the media, long before any formal judicial verdicts were handed down. And finally, despite an explicit provision in the new code of criminal procedure calling for public access to criminal trials, the trial of the "gang" was closed to all but a small number of hand picked observers--this on the grounds that the probable exposure of several "important state secrets" overrode the principle of public access.

Despite these problems, the trial was a significant--albeit imperfect--move in the direction of socialist legality. The very fact that the four "gang" leaders appeared in a publicly reported court session was in marked contrast with the Cultural Revolution period when they held sway. Their case was generally handled in accordance with newly articulated legal norms, including the principle of formal indictment and the rights of the accused to be represented by counsel and to cross-examine prosecution witnesses.

"Due process" aside, the case against the members of the "gang" centered on allegations concerning their repeated attempts to discredit and persecute political opponents, and thereby effect a seizure of power, during China's "decade of destruction" (1966-76). Directly or indirectly, they were said to be responsible for causing the deaths of 34,800 people and the wrongful persecution and torture of 726,000 others in the first eighteen months of the Cultural Revolution. (Staggering as these figure are, it has been unofficially estimated that several times as many people may have been killed or physically abused in China between 1966 and 1968, the years of greatest violence. That the number of victims cited in the official indictment was thus on the conservative side was said to be the result of the government's attempt to individually document each case of wrongful persecution, torture, and homicide.)

In addition to charges stemming from their alleged criminal activities during the early years of the Cultural Revolution, the "gang" also stood accused of:

—hatching a "counterrevolutionary plot" in 1974-75 to discredit Premier Zhou Enlai and prevent Zhou's protege, Deng Xiaoping, from making a political comeback;

—plotting to overthrow Deng on trumped-up charges of being an "unrepentant capitalist roader" in the aftermath of the Tiananmen Incident of April 1976;

—plotting to stage an "armed rebellion" in Shanghai in October 1976, shortly after Mao's death, as prelude to an attempted power seizure.

A partial listing in the indictment of the alleged

victims of gang-inspired persecutions and frame-ups read like a virtual "who's who" of top Chinese Party and government leaders. Headed by Liu Shaoqi and Deng Xiaoping, the list included twenty past or present members of the Central Committee Politburo; eighty-eight full or alternate members of the Central Committee; twelve vice premiers of the State Council; five vice chairmen of the Party Military Affairs Commission; thirteen members of the Central Party Secretariat; four first secretaries of Party regional bureaus; and eighty-three other high-ranking Party, government, and military officials--a formidable "hit list" indeed.

The trial itself began amidst great public fanfare on November 20. In lieu of direct public access to the proceedings, carefully edited film clips from the trial were shown nightly on Chinese television. Lengthy excerpts were also published daily in the official press.

Represented in court by ten defense attorneys, and carefully coached in advance by government prosecutors, most of the defendants, after being presented with graphic--and in some cases grisly--evidence of their alleged crimes, in due course admitted guilt and begged for mercy from the court. Some were more recalcitrant than others, however; and at least one defendant adamantly refused to knuckle under to government pressure.

Jiang Qing hears the testimony of a former associate, Wang Hongwen. (Eastfoto)

To the very end, Jiang Qing, acting as her own defense attorney, head held high in a studied gesture of defiance reminiscent of her youthful career as an aspiring actress, steadfastly denied her guilt. Denouncing prosecution witnesses as "traitors," she derided the court and challenged the very legitimacy of the government. On two occasions Jiang was ejected from the courtroom after engaging in heated shouting matches with witnesses, judges, and prosecutors alike.

Despite the government's public commitment to new legal norms, the outcome of the trial was never seriously in doubt. The only remaining question concerned the severity of the sentences. Following a post-trial delay of several weeks, during which the thirty-five judges reportedly consulted with Party and government leaders on the question of sentencing, the unrepentant Jiang Qing and her principal coconspirator, Zhang Chunqiao, were given suspended death sentences, with the possibility of commutation to life imprisonment after two years for sincere repentance. Other "gang" members, as well as the surviving leaders of the "Lin Biao clique," drew lengthy prison sentences ranging from sixteen years to life.

THE EMPTY PLACE IN THE DOCK

Perhaps more significant than what did happen during the six-week trial was what did not happen. For among the deceased, unindicted coconspirators who tacitly stood in the dock alongside the "gang of four," only one--Chairman Mao--escaped criminal judgment.

No formal charges had been filed against Mao, and no indictment sought; no witnesses were called to denounce him, and no verdict rendered. As if to underscore the fact that Mao was being carefully shielded at the trial from implication in the evil deeds of the "gang," an official media commentary published in late December unequivocally asserted that the trial "has nothing to do with Mao Zedong's responsibility or his contributions and mistakes. His mistakes are entirely different from the crimes of the gang."

Despite such pointed disclaimers, however, the silent specter of the late chairman hung over the trial. The silence was deafening.

Clearly, Mao was on trial--at least in the minds of many. For it was Mao who had launched the "disastrous" Cultural Revolution; Mao who had recruited the "gang of four" and appointed three of their number--Jiang, Zhang, and Yao--to direct the purge of "capitalist roaders" in the Party; Mao who had urged the youthful Red Guards to "bombard the headquarters"; Mao who had sealed the fate of Liu Shaoqi as a "renegade, traitor, and scab"; and Mao who had ordered Deng Xiaoping dismissed from office as a "counterrevolutionary" following the Tiananmen Incident

of April 1976.
Watching the authorized film clips and listening to the parade of cultural revolutionary horrors described in the vivid testimonies of dozens of victims of radical persecution, terror, and brutality, a shocked Chinese public could hardly avoid posing the obvious question: "How could this have happened?"
Indeed, this was precisely the question that Jiang Qing sought to plant in the public mind throughout the trial. Alone among the defendants, Mao's widow had raised the classic Nuremberg Defense: "I was only following orders." By sticking to this line throughout, Jiang sought to make Mao and his policies her basic line of defense.
The government countered by insisting that the gang's "crimes" had nothing to do with Mao's "mistakes." But it had a hollow ring to it. Jiang had succeeded in making her point--though it might still cost her her life. Sooner or later, the unclear distinction between "mistakes" and "crimes" would have to be squarely addressed; and most observers expected this to come at a Party Central Committee meeting scheduled for spring 1981, where the question of Hua Guofeng's political future was also due to be decided.

AFTERMATH

The inevitable conviction of the "gang" ostensibly cleared the way for enlarging the scope of judicial retribution in China, as hundreds of other former radical leaders of the Cultural Revolution were expected to face trial on various charges of "counterrevolutionary activity." At least sixty codefendants had been named during the trial of the "gang," including Mao's nephew, Mao Yuanxin, a fomer Party leader in Liaoning Province, and former Shanghai mayor Ma Tianshui.
According to unofficial Chinese sources, more than 600 alleged followers of the "gang of four" were under arrest in Shanghai at year's end, with similar figures being reported from other parts of the country.
While the potential for continued political bloodletting was thus undeniably high, many observers expected the new regime to limit the scope of the second wave of trials out of concern for preserving the fragile "stability and unity" of the country. Thus, according to one Chinese official the "basic criterion" for the new round of trials "should be justice, not vengeance."
Of particular concern for the regime of Deng Xiaoping, Zhao Ziyang, and Hu Yaobang was the possibility that excessive recrimination against Cultural Revolution radicals might stir up a substantial political backlash among millions of ordinary Chinese cadres who had survived the traumas of the Cultural Revolution. Many of

these survivors had gone along with the radicals in order to save--or advance--their own careers. Understandably, they had little enthusiasm for a new vendetta; and there was thus a danger that the regime might overplay its hand if it chose to extract a full pound of flesh from all erstwhile "ultraleftists."

Then, too, there was the very real possibility that Deng might overplay his own personal hand to secure the ouster of Chairman Hua Guofeng. At year's end there were widespread reports that various Party leaders were trying to persuade the tenacious, revenge-minded Deng to compromise his differences with Hua rather than force a divisive final showdown. Thus, in the last week of 1980, the Party's ideological journal, Red Flag, published an allegorical commentary concerning a personal grudge once held by an elderly Chinese general against a younger minister. Noting with approval the fact that the old general eventually acknowledged the error of his desire for vengeance and thereafter worked with the minister for the good of the country, the commentary drew from this parable the following moral lesson: "You must have a large heart and not hold a grudge."

To say that China's stability and unity depended upon the largeness of Deng Xiaoping's heart would undoubtedly be an overstatement; yet there were clear signs that Deng was being strongly urged by his comrades to call off his personal vendetta against Hua and the remnants of the cultural revolutionary Left. Whether the crusty veteran of China's political wars would bow to such pressures was unclear as 1981 began.

Clearer by far was the extreme fragility of China's newborn socialist democracy and the extreme immaturity of China's rudimentary rule of law. The crisis of public confidence that had called forth these radical innovations had been weathered, at least for the time being. But the reforms themselves had not yet irreversibly taken root; and any further political destabilization could easily jeopardize their future viability. Under the circumstances, the admonition to "have a large heart and not hold a grudge" seemed sound advice indeed.

4
The Chinese Economy in 1980: Death of Reform?

Bruce L. Reynolds

INTRODUCTION

In late 1980 and early 1981 there was little good economic news out of China. Among the gloomy reports:
--Bad weather brought a decline in grain output. In the drought-stricken northern plain and the waterlogged central Yangzi valley, the shortages were serious enough to cause some malnutrition. China broke a thirty-year tradition and asked for United Nations assistance.
--A large deficit in the central government budget, low foreign exchange reserves, and stagnant petroleum supplies forced the suspension of several major development projects in which foreign firms were involved. To help deal with the balance-of-payments deficit, China secured a $550 million loan from the International Monetary Fund.
--Exceptional inflation, the unintended consequence of several new economic policies, created some discontent in China's cities, aggravated by memories of the hyperinflation of the late 1940s.
It should be emphasized that there is no danger of economic collapse. Indeed, there appears to be a gradual improvement in general living standards. But past optimism regarding China's economic potential was clearly unfounded, and Deng Xiaoping and his associates face serious problems ahead.
Behind the headlines is another story: China's leaders have created for themselves a conflict between economic priorities and economic structure. In 1979 they adopted a two-pronged policy of economic development that contrasted sharply with past approaches. The first prong was "readjustment," allocating less resources to new industrial plant and more to consumer goods for both domestic and foreign markets. To facilitate this new orientation, they experimented with "restructuring," liberalization of the country's central planning system. The rationale for pursuing both at once was sensible:

factories could not adequately meet consumers' needs without greater independence to make decisions and better knowledge of product demand.

By the end of 1980, however, the second part of the strategy--actually an experiment with market socialism--had to be downgraded. Decentralization was contributing to inflation, and central planning won a new lease on life.

Deng and his colleagues are now caught in a bind. They remain committed to raising living standards, fearing the kind of labor unrest that has plagued Poland. However, central planning seems ill-equipped to meet the demand for consumer goods. Three options are available: muddling through, returning to a strategy that emphasizes heavy industry, or overhauling the entire economic system.

THE READJUSTMENT STRATEGY: RATIONALE AND PITFALLS

At first glance, "economic readjustment" would seem to be unnecessary in China. From 1950 to 1980 the gross national product (GNP) grew at roughly 6 percent per year, comparable to other developing countries. China's per capita output of steel and electricity is on par with that of Thailand and the Philippines. It is the fifth largest steel producer in the world, and its total production of cotton yarn exceeds that of the United States and the Soviet Union combined. China has also made significant progress in providing its people with basic necessities and in reducing income inequality.

But this economic success story was written at tremendous cost. Because of population growth and a concentration of investment in heavy industry, living standards stagnated after 1957, depressing labor productivity. For example, average per capita food grain supplies were lower in 1977 than two decades before, and the share of calories from noncereal sources was the lowest in Asia. Per capita supplies of cotton cloth--still a rationed commodity--grew by only a third during the same period. The housing supply declined in both quality and per capita quantity. Energy supplies and transportation facilities were strained to the limit, creating further strains.

To rectify these imbalances, China's leaders began considering "economic readjustment" in late 1978 (this only months after they had adopted a policy of rapid expansion of heavy industry). The new strategy had two principal components: reducing investment to raise consumption, and shifting the remaining investment resources toward the production of consumer goods.

Even in a short period, the new policy has borne considerable results. Whereas state investment increased by a massive 31.3 percent in 1978 on top of a sizable increase in 1977, it grew only 4.4 percent in 1979 and not at all in 1980. As a result, total investment as a proportion of gross national product declined from 36.5 percent in 1978 to perhaps 30 percent in 1980. Although a modest increase in the absolute level of investment is planned for 1981, the investment-to-GNP ratio is to remain below 30 percent after that. Industry is to grow at 6 percent per year--less than the 10 percent rate since 1952 but still quite respectable.

In reducing the level of investment, China's leaders were banking on a rapid increase in living standards in a short period of time. They predicted that because the producer goods sector (steel, coal, etc.) was already producing more than enough to sustain 6 percent growth in industry overall, light industry could grow quickly without new investment in heavy industry. Indeed, while heavy industry grew hardly at all in 1980, output of textiles and other consumer goods rose by a startling 18.4 percent.

Despite this initial success, China still faces a number of economic problems. Some are the result of resource imbalances (food, energy, jobs), while others stem directly from the prevailing economic system.

First of all, the payoff of increased consumer goods from a reallocation of investment is neither automatic nor permanent. Shifting gears in a bureaucratic planning system is not a frictionless operation. Some grinding inevitably occurs, reducing the size of the "readjustment dividend." After 1982, moreover, the slack in the producer goods sector will disappear completely. Satisfying the country's whetted appetite for consumer goods will then have to be achieved in other, less easy ways-- increased industrial productivity, modernization in agriculture, and dynamic growth in the export sector.

Second, a stagnation in energy supplies will soon create bottlenecks. Total energy production for 1980 dropped 2.9 percent, with coal and crude oil output declining and electricity growing at a modest 6.6 percent. In the short term this shortfall will not create serious shortages because the energy-intensive producer goods sector occupies a declining share of industrial production. Thus industrial output grew by 8.4 percent in 1980, while energy output declined by almost 3 percent. (Usually each 1 percent gain in industrial output has required a 1.2 percent increase in energy output.) Satisfying long-term needs is another matter, and the government seems to be wasting the breathing space provided by this relative decline in energy demand. For example, although a severe electricity shortage in 1979-80 idled factory capacity, the Three Gorges hydroelectric project on the Yangzi River was postponed, raising questions about long-term sources of new generating capacity.

Third, agriculture also fared poorly in 1980, but appears to face a somewhat brighter future. Grain output fell 4.8 percent short of the 1979 record, due mainly to exceptionally bad weather. Output of nongrain commodities increased, but not as much as had been hoped; cotton and sugar, for example, fell short of their targets. All this means continued high agricultural imports, siphoning off valuable foreign exchange.

Still, agriculture in 1980 could not have hoped to match the very rapid increases of the previous three years and should bounce back in 1981. Growth over the long term will depend on a continued heavy flow of resources from the industrial sector (machinery, chemical fertilizer) and application of agricultural technologies already in use in Japan and elsewhere. If these things occur, the next decade should see Chinese rice yields rising by 50 percent and wheat and maize yields by 25 to 50 percent.

Fourth, budget deficits have fed inflation. The Chinese government ran large deficits in 1978, 1979, and 1980, and anticipates another one in 1981 (though the size of the gap has narrowed). As a result, consumer prices in urban areas rose roughly 6 percent in 1979 and 1980, according to official statistics. The government has rationalized the deficits as the cost of achieving other important goals, such as compensating victims of the Cultural Revolution. Continued inflation could generate further social friction and erode the government's political base. Recent policy statements in December have revealed a deep anxiety on this score.

Fifth, urban unemployment is a continuing problem. In the later years of the Cultural Revolution, some ten to fifteen million high school graduates were "sent down" to the countryside for more-or-less permanent resettlement. This had only a limited effect, since a migration into cities of comparable magnitude was permitted in the same period, and large numbers of "rusticated" youth found their way back to their urban homes.

Energetic efforts in 1979 and 1980 apparently succeeded in nearly eliminating the backlog of "youths awaiting employment," but the pressure to create new jobs will persist. In every year of the 1980s at least 3.5 million high school graduates will be looking for work or entrance to universities, with the numbers rising to 4 million in 1986-88 (reflecting the relaxation of the birth control program during the first convulsive years of the Cultural Revolution). To absorb these additions to the labor force and simultaneously generate employment in rural areas, the government must channel new investment to sectors where the ratio of labor to capital is high. As one Chinese economist writes:

Greater attention should be paid to developing those [industries] with low technical composition and higher labor intensity, capable of absorbing more workers, especially those crafts and arts products [which] find a good international market. In doing so, we can not only expand employment, but also bring into play on the international market such advantages as our rich labor resource, low wage cost and traditional craftsmanship.

Finally, and most relevant to the issue of economic structure, are the related problems of low product quality and low labor productivity, the inevitable results of China's past system of industrial management. With the government setting wage rates and siphoning off all of an enterprise's profits (net income), factory managers lacked the authority to foster productivity through salary increases, bonuses, and employee welfare services. Nor did they have any incentive to improve product quality, since they were judged on the basis of their factory's output rather than the cost of production or the value to the eventual user. As one factory manager said when asked about the crates of surplus merchandise rusting in the courtyard of his factory, "Once it's outside the factory's door, it's the state's responsibility."

Deng Xiaoping and his associates soon decided that major changes in the system of industrial management were necessary to facilitate the "readjustment" policies and long-term growth as well. They had hoped that deemphasizing ideological motivation and raising workers' wages would enhance productivity. But increased incomes would enhance productivity only if there were goods of adequate quality for workers to buy. Inattention to quality and user specifications might have been acceptable when a factory's principal customers were other enterprises. But such defects were not acceptable to Chinese consumers--and foreign buyers--who now wanted bicycles that worked, shoes that fit, and even a bit of styling.

THE TRANSITION TO AN EXPORT-ORIENTED ECONOMY

At the same time China's post-Mao leaders were changing internal economic policies, they were also altering China's approach to international trade. They shifted the emphasis from the import of advanced technology embodied in whole plants to the high-volume export of consumer goods. In the process more questions were raised about the effectiveness of the central planning system.

China's initial closed-door approach to international trade after 1949 was a response to circumstances. For reasons of nationalism and security, the new

Communist leaders wanted to industrialize rapidly. But they also faced a Western trade embargo. Not surprisingly, they adopted a policy of developing domestic industries that would substitute for imports, beginning with consumer goods and then moving to producer goods of increasing sophistication. Such a policy is sometimes called "autarky" or, in the Chinese lexicon, "self-reliance."

Under this policy--import whatever is needed to reduce imports, and export only what is needed to pay for imports--Chinese foreign trade atrophied, falling from a world share of 1.4 percent in the 1950s to 1.1 percent in the 1960s and 0.8 percent in the 1970s. Even by 1979 exports were only 3-4 percent of China's total GNP, a low proportion for a large, continental economy. The composition of imports was four-fifths producer goods and one-fifth consumer goods (principally grain). China ignored the possibilities for international specialization, and instead produced at home everything which could be produced there, regardless of cost.

Import substitution only makes sense when restricted to consumer nondurables such as textiles and processed foods. These products are labor intensive, and thus appropriate to the labor-rich developing countries. Extending the policy to intermediate and final producer goods went against China's comparative advantage, for it was unlikely that China could produce these capital-intensive goods more cheaply there than in Japan and the West. Other countries' experience bears this out. A number of Latin American countries tried import substitution after World War II and performed poorly. By contrast, Korea, Taiwan, Hong Kong, and Singapore successfully used export promotion to rapidly increase both GNP and living standards.

Even the threat of protectionism in the developed economies does not seem to pose an obstacle to an export-led growth strategy. Recent studies estimate that developed countries can absorb 12.5 percent more manufactured consumer goods from less-developed countries without excessively threatening employment. By 1990 such imports would still constitute only 4 percent of the manufactures consumed by developed countries. China's exports of manufactures represent only one-twelfth of all developing country exports. Thus China can probably expand its manufactured exports faster than the 12.5 percent rate, especially since most of China's manufactures go to other less-developed countries anyway.

Apparently recognizing the logic of these numbers, the government in 1980 expanded China's involvement in the international economy by:

--opening the twenty ports in Fujian Province and all the major Yangzi River ports to international trade.

--creating special tariff-free zones for processing

A worker in a ceramics factory in Foshan (outside Guangzhou). Most of the factory's output is exported.

and re-export in Guangdong near Hong Kong, and at three sites in Fujian.

--concluding textile agreements with the United States and the European Economic Community, agreements which leave her ample room to expand exports.

--joining the International Monetary Fund and the World Bank.

--moving toward becoming a party to the General Agreements of Trade and Tariffs, principally, one suspects, to secure the low General System of Preferences tariff rates for exports to the US.

The trade figures for 1980 also confirm a shift in foreign trade policy, toward an approach more suited to labor-intensive manufactured consumer goods. In real terms, exports grew by 14.3 percent while imports grew by only 2.1 percent.

China's leaders went further than reorienting trade policy. They began asking whether the existing economic system could accommodate itself to even a limited expansion of foreign trade.* Foreign trade had been a central

---

*Still unanswered is whether economic planners have become sufficiently aware of China's comparative disadvantage in some producer goods--particularly in intermediate goods using highly automated flow-technology processes--to reverse the policy of self-reliance in those areas as well.

government monopoly, with all contracts negotiated by ministries in Beijing. Could the central government effectively coordinate and guide the thousands or tens of thousands of small enterprises that would produce labor-intensive exports? When quality and a precise understanding of buyers' specifications were crucial, as in the fierce competition of international trade, should not Chinese producers be in direct contact with foreign buyers? Could the new emphasis on export goods, like the new emphasis on consumer goods for domestic markets, be implemented without reform of the industrial structure?

ECONOMIC REFORMS IN INDUSTRY

China's industry, like that of the US, has two distinct sectors. A relatively small number of large, state-owned enterprises produces most of the industrial output while a large number of smaller, collectively owned enterprises produce the rest. Workers in the large factories are complemented by a relatively large amount of capital and are therefore more productive.

As of the late 1970s, government control varied with enterprise size and output. The state controlled the very large, very productive enterprises, most of them built through state investment in the first place. Central ministries in Beijing have controlled the largest 4,400, and provincial governments another 40,000. The peripheral, labor-intensive enterprises, whose sheer numbers would defeat any attempt at central planning, were left to fend for themselves.

The government also allocated key producer goods, invariably inputs in short supply such as electricity. There were 256 items so rationed in 1979. State enterprises applied for these goods through their parent ministries. Collective enterprises scrambled to purchase what was left over, available only through the ministry of commerce.

Unlike market economies, the Chinese banking system and price structure played a passive role. Banks provided capital to enterprises not on the basis of enterprise profitability but in response to administrative orders from above. The state fixed prices for key producer goods and rarely changed them (most prices were set in 1970). The most obvious example of a frozen, passive price was the overvalued dollar price of China's currency, the yuan. This artificial exchange rate made most potential imports seem attractive, and most exports unprofitable.

In short, economic decisions were made by administrative fiat. Through direct control over a relatively small number of factories, ministries decided what should be produced, provided the incentives and, through the state materials bureau, allocated raw materials.

Given such a structure, what are the consequences of emphasizing consumer goods over producer goods, of promoting exports rather than substituting for imports? If smaller enterprises, not necessarily state owned, are best suited to such a policy, can administrative channels provide the sufficient information, incentives, and physical and financial resources?

The Chinese leadership answered in the negative, concluding that its strategy for growth was unworkable without reform of the economic structure.* In late 1979 and early 1980 it took a number of significant steps:

--It strengthened the role of the profit motive in production and the market mechanism in distribution.

--It relaxed somewhat the center's fierce grip on key supplies (the number of centrally rationed commodities was to be reduced by at least 70 percent by 1981).

--It allowed local banks some autonomy in extending credit.

--It gave local governments and enterprises more financial freedom.

Experiments with enterprise management illustrate the scope of the reforms. In July 1979, 4,000 state-owned enterprises were allowed to retain on a trial basis 20 percent of the profits they would have normally remitted to the state (four billion yuan). This change was extended to 6,600 enterprises in 1980, and was scheduled to go into effect in all state enterprises in 1981. Fulfillment of orders--whether an enterprise met buyers' specifications--was another new criterion for evaluating managers. When state trading companies refused to automatically buy useless or overstocked goods, factory salesmen reportedly fanned out frantically across the country.

The government also increased incentives for producing goods for export. No longer would all foreign exchange earned from exports have to be remitted to the central government. As of early 1979, a province which increased its foreign exchange earnings could retain roughly 40 percent of its enterprises' export earnings, to be shared among the provincial, prefectural, and certain municipal governments, as well as certain major enterprises.

---

*A Western "bourgeois" economist would concur in that conclusion. That is, information on what to produce is best conveyed indirectly, through market prices of both commodities and the currency. Incentives should also be indirect, based on profits. And central allocation of producer goods and bank credit must also be relaxed, especially if the peripheral, collective sector is to play a larger role.

A worker in a Guangzhou machine tool factory, one of many that received "expanded self-management powers" in 1979-80.

The government also allowed enterprises to negotiate foreign trade contracts directly (although the supervision and final approval of higher-level authorities was presumably still required). The Bank of China made available through its local branches two billion yuan in foreign exchange for the expansion of export-oriented enterprises. And the yuan was devalued by almost 50 percent in late 1980.

In some respects, however, the reforms did not go far enough. Serious problems emerged because markets were not used broadly enough to generate prices and to convey information about demand. Prices, most still set by the state, were uncertain indicators of the true scarcity of goods when fixed in 1970, and are even less informative now. Adjustments made in 1980 were only a small first step in rectifying the problem. In the meantime, calculating profits in terms of those prices will be a poor indication of efficient production and guidance concerning future investment.

More distressing was the reemergence of inflation for the first time since the early 1950s, recalling the economic collapse of the last days of Chiang Kai-shek's Nationalists. As part of the 1979 reform package, the government allowed factories to sell, directly and at negotiated prices, any output that exceeded their annual target (a similar provision was adopted for grain sales by peasants). But negotiated prices, naturally enough, tended to be higher than state prices. Shortages of key supplies and unauthorized construction (which increased state expenditures) aggravated the situation. In early December 1980 an alarmed government moved to end the unintended consequences of reform.

DECEMBER 1980: RETREAT FROM REFORM

A People's Daily editorial on December 2 signalled the death, or at least the suspension, of the reform movement, calling for "a necessary and adequate retreat" from the experiments. "Powers of self-management" will apparently not be extended to all state enterprises in 1981 as planned. Those enterprises now enjoying such powers may lose them. Enterprises will no longer have the power to expand capacity using their own funds. New construction by local governments will be closely controlled by Beijing. The relaxation of the central supply system may well be reversed, and much stricter control of prices has already begun.

What so alarmed China's leaders? They learned, to their dismay, that factories given new freedoms used them in ways the center opposed. Many local plants took advantage of relaxed credit controls by expanding their capacity to produce consumer goods. In principle, this was in line with official policy of raising consumption, and it was profitable, given China's price structure. But in a number of product lines, it was not productive capacity that was lacking but raw materials and power. The unnecessary building of new plants only diverted raw materials from existing factories, forcing them to stand idle. It siphoned off resources from other goals, such as the construction of desperately needed new housing. In rural areas, peasants began to sell their goods at higher, "negotiated" prices before, not after, fulfilling their contracts with the state. Snowballing inflation was the result.

Those Chinese leaders who favor more independent enterprises and a guided market system say that the reforms have been postponed, not abandoned. Their program will continue, they claim, once the "readjustment" program rectifies the imbalances in supply and demand that the reforms made obvious. An advocate of market socialism, the senior economist Xue Muqiao said in March 1981:

> Particularly strict management is necessary when the national economy is in dislocation. For this reason, this year, more controls will be applied to locally run medium and small-scale enterprises and the extent of centralization will be slightly

greater than in the past two years. . . . [But] this is only a temporary measure.

As they see it, China's planners are in the role of a driving instructor who must insure that the car is in the middle of the road, pointing the right way, and not moving too fast before letting an inexperienced driver take the wheel.
This optimistic view is based on a questionable assumption: that the road to market socialism is unobstructed, that both central planners and plant managers have the information they need to make correct decisions. They may be more like men piling up bricks in the dark, who learn which tower needs shoring only from the sound of the crash as it collapses to the floor. Expanding the role of market forces in 1980 was like turning on the lights. The leadership saw chaos and possible collapse, and retreated from the brink.

CONCLUSION

For eighteen months--from mid-1979 to late 1980--China's leaders engaged in a daring yet partial experiment to accommodate the country's economic structure to the new goals of increased domestic consumption and expanded exports. They began grafting onto a centrally planned system institutions with a strong market flavor:
--banks that would evaluate and control investment through loan policies.
--state-owned factories that would have the independence and initiative to respond to domestic and foreign demand.
--peasants who would work collectively but in response to price incentives.
By early 1981 it seemed clear that the experiment had not worked. The goals will remain, primarily because the leadership has bet its political fortune on rising living standards. But for the immediate future there will be a substantial role for central planning.
This approach may prove quite successful, but there will be a price. Without a new effort at reform, the industrial system will remain overcapitalized, inefficient, and ill-equipped to modernize agriculture or take full advantage of international trade. Whether the leadership will accept that price or risk broader structural change is another question.

5
Youth in China Today: Obstacle to Economic Modernization?

Thomas B. Gold

"We never questioned anything. But not anymore."

"There's a real malaise among the workers. Young people are turned off."

"The management is a mess. There is a tremendous gap between labor and management."

"Workers don't think in terms of an abstract 'system.' What matters to them is having enough to eat and wear, a television, a radio, and a sewing machine. They know and care little about Marxism-Leninism."

"I like country and western music. Do you have any Dolly Parton tapes?"

These are a few voices of alienated youth in China. Lacking a Chinese Gallup Poll, it is impossible to know precisely how widespread such sentiments are. But at a time of major transition, when even late Party Chairman Mao Zedong is the object of official criticism, it is apparent that a serious problem exists, particularly among urban young people. Perhaps the best evidence is that the government has publicly acknowledged the situation and the possible implications for its ambitious economic development goals.

The average age in China is twenty-six, and 65 percent of the population of one billion is under thirty years old. There are an estimated 160 million people, now twenty-two to thirty-three, born during the first decade of Communist rule. The teenage population is around 210 million, almost as large as the total population of the United States. If the leadership is to achieve the four modernizations (of agriculture, industry, science and technology, and national defense), it must somehow secure the commitment of this youth

generation.
How widespread is the alienation of adolescents and young adults in China? What are its sources and how is it expressed? How is the government dealing with it? How will it affect China's developmental effort?

I have heard partial answers to these questions. I lived and traveled in China from early 1979 to early 1980 as an exchange student at Fudan University in Shanghai, and have served as an interpreter for Chinese visiting the United States (many of whom I saw again in China). My contacts were primarily city-dwellers, whereas most Chinese, young people included, live in rural areas. Even so, urban youth are increasingly important in Chinese politics. These are their voices.

THE GENERAL SITUATION OF URBAN YOUTH

As a rule, young people in China's cities share several common problems. Their situation is not unique, existing in other developing and developed countries. But it has special features in China because of the country's recent self-inflicted turmoil, particularly the Cultural Revolution which began in 1966, and the intense political struggles that preceded the death of Mao Zedong in 1976.*

Two decades of political conflict have left urban young people alienated and cynical. They have watched one political faction after another come to power and vigorously promote certain policies, only to be toppled by a new group that promotes its own vision and castigates that of its predecessor. Growing public criticism of Mao Zedong--and its implications for the Communist system's legitimacy--will only confirm their general skepticism of authority.

Urban youth are for the most part poorly educated and lack discipline. The Cultural Revolution crippled the educational system and shattered social order. During the years of greatest turmoil (1966-68), student Red Guards followed Mao's dictum that "to rebel is justified," and teachers became the targets of mass criticism. Subsequently, there was only a partial restoration of discipline in schools and in society as a whole. It is no coincidence that recent government efforts to reduce the urban crime rate have netted a fairly large proportion of young people.

In both city and countryside, Chinese youth have over the last decade endured limited employment opportunities and a stagnant standard of living. Although the

─────────────

*Whether rural youth share these problems is unclear; little information exists concerning their attitudes.

government no longer compels urban youth to work in the countryside (as it did in the 1970s), the current alternatives still leave much to be desired. Young people are either assigned randomly to jobs where their talents are often not utilized, or shunted into "collective" (nonstate) employment where wages and benefits are relatively low. Some high school graduates must wait more than a year for their assignments. Generally, rural youth are not allowed to seek urban jobs and must stay in their home villages. The government has tried to improve consumer welfare, but not fast enough to match expectations inflated by contact with the outside world and the regime's own propaganda.

Finally, urban youth, like other Chinese, must cope with a doubly heavy hand of the state. On the one hand, officialdom interferes in nearly all aspects of life, even some that Americans would consider very personal. On the other, officials are loathe to take much initiative. Party cadres, remembering past political turmoil, are fearful that any action they take today will bring them trouble tomorrow. Often defying official Party policy, they ignore or stifle suggestions from subordinates or other citizens. The result has been a wide split between leaders and led, and between Party members and non-members.

TYPES OF URBAN YOUTH

While generally sharing these problems, Chinese urban youth can be subdivided into three groups, based on age. The first consists of those around thirty, the second is teenagers and those in their early twenties, and the third includes those in their mid-to-late twenties. Each group has distinct experiences which affect its position in society and its outlook on the current political and economic situation.

The Former Red Guards

The same age as the People's Republic, the Red Guards spent their formative years during the period of great revolutionary optimism and elan. And they have borne the brunt of one policy twist and turn after another.

One member of this subgeneration, now a nationally prominent performer, described the origins of the Red Guards' political activism:

> As children, we were loyal to the Party and Chairman Mao because they gave us social stability, security, and opportunities for the future that those who grew up before Liberation [1949] never knew. We forgave them for the hardships of the Great Leap Forward,

and plunged eagerly into the Cultural Revolution when we thought Chairman Mao was under attack. We never questioned anything. But not anymore.

For China, the Cultural Revolution soon brought chaos, as Red Guards joined various contending factions, each claiming to protect Mao's road to communism. After two years of turmoil, the army was called in to stop the Red Guards' destructive rampages, urging them to go to the countryside among the peasant masses. Many joined this mass movement, which was also designed to reduce urban unemployment, increase agricultural production, and raise the educational level in rural areas. Most were to settle for life, held in place by the official strictures on internal migration.

The hardships of rural life, sometimes in China's remotest regions, combined with a generally cool reception from the peasants, quickly dulled the appeal of going "up to the mountains and down to the countryside." Only a small proportion were able to maintain their original commitment. Others found ways of leaving: gaining admission to urban schools, finding a job in the city, seeking medical treatment, or fabricating other excuses. Many of those who remained in the countryside came to believe they had been tricked and then abandoned, especially when Mao's successors blamed them for the excesses of the Cultural Revolution.

The few who returned to enter universities did not always like what they found. The experience of a thirty-two-year-old Fudan University sophomore, who had done stints as a Red Guard, commune peasant, and dock worker before matriculating in 1977, is typical. He is interested in his courses but feels that the teachers are still afraid to teach. His classmates talk, write, or knit rather than listen to the teacher read officially approved textbooks. Given a choice, he would rather study architecture at another school, but transferring is virtually impossible. He is desperately trying to make up for ten years of lost time by voraciously reading, questioning, and writing. He has little faith in the current system yet wants to improve himself and make a contribution to society.

Large numbers of former Red Guards stranded in the countryside saw an opportunity to return to the cities when the political situation relaxed in late 1978 and open dissent appeared on "democracy walls." Having come home for the spring festival (celebrated at the time of traditional Chinese New Year), they refused to return and took to the streets to make their point. In one such demonstration on March 15, 1979, a crowd of returnees waving banners and shouting slogans blocked the entrance to the Shanghai concert hall parking lot just as members of the Boston Symphony Orchestra approached in a motorcade. They sought to publicize their desire to remain in Shanghai rather than return to the far-off border regions where they had been sent in 1968. Their spokesman, a thirty-year-old orphan, stated their case to the assembled foreign journalists and onlookers:

> During the height of the Cultural Revolution, we volunteered to commit the rest of our lives to help build socialism in the border areas. Now we are disillusioned, feeling our lives were sacrificed in the interests of a national power struggle. Shorn of our idealism, we found the hard physical labor, the primitive work methods, the spartan living conditions, the low wages, and the abuse by cadres increasingly unbearable. We are without the connections or money that others used to get themselves back to the relative ease of city life. During the Chinese New Year's vacation, we came home to Shanghai determined to find a way to stay.*

Forced to return to the countryside, many could not stay. They, like most former Red Guards, have formed a lost generation. But they are often politically astute and articulate. One university student observed, "What characterizes people of our generation is that we learned to think on our own as a result of experiencing the Cultural Revolution." They have seen that they cannot satisfy most of their demands through the system and are experienced at using disruptive tactics to gain attention. Recent reports suggest that demonstrations and other forms of overt political activity--including violence--are continuing. The former Red Guards thus remain a threat to political stability and a potential obstacle to the modernization program.

Teenagers

This group, the youngest of the three, stands in marked contrast to the Red Guard generation. Those around thirty spent their earliest years in a relatively stable environment and received several years of schooling prior to the upheavals of the 1960s. The teenagers were born at the height of the chaos and got less formal education or moral training. The thirty-year-olds went to China's backward areas for social service, but most of today's teenagers can pass directly from high school to university or urban employment without interruption. As a result, many teenagers seem to lack a social conscience or sense of higher purpose. They believe that hard work will pay off in good jobs and financial and political

---

*These remarks are paraphrased.

security. Politics, they feel, is dangerous, so they channel their energies into schoolwork. (In so doing they earn the disdain of the former Red Guards, many of whom feel, in the words of one, that, "These teenagers are useless. All they can do is memorize books and repeat by rote.")

But few in their late teens or early twenties can realistically expect either a university education or employment in state-run organizations, which provide relatively high wages, bonuses, and welfare benefits. Only about one percent of the college-age population will be enrolled. Past economic dislocation and rapid population growth have severely limited the creation of new jobs in the state sector.

To avoid the twin evils of urban unemployment and sending large numbers of high school graduates to the countryside against their will, the government is now channeling urban youth into hastily created "collective" enterprises, specializing in handicrafts and services. Those so employed have little choice in their assignment. They receive wages and welfare benefits that generally lag behind those of state firms. Not surprisingly, many take an indifferent and sullen attitude toward their jobs.

Young university students specializing in English, like these students at Liaoning University, have the best chance of securing good jobs.

A seventeen-year-old male in the eastern city of Yangzhou described his situation:

> I've been in the appliance factory for three months now. As far as factories go it's okay, but there is a real malaise among the workers. Young people are really turned off and you can't mobilize anybody to work for the four modernizations. They've been fooled too long. People aren't so simple anymore. We all talk about these things together, but never when the leaders are around or at study sessions. Some people are activists but everyone suspects their motives. They want to accumulate political capital so they can enter the Youth League or Party and then share in all sorts of special privileges that go with it. There's really so little else anyone can hope to share in in this country.

This disaffection is sometimes expressed more overtly, through political outlets and also through crime. Individuals in their late teens and early twenties participated actively in the Democracy Movement of 1978-79, spending evenings reading or writing wall posters and listening to speeches. But an alarming number of people in this generation are turning to crime and hooliganism. People in some cities are afraid to go out alone at night. Citizens have organized night patrols to combat the lawlessness, and teenage crime is a principal target of the authorities' effort to restore law and order.

How to handle teenagers whose entire lives have been spent in a society with indefinite rules has been a subject of widespread discussion. In "Class Counselor," a popular short story by Liu Xinwu, a teacher accepts a juvenile delinquent into his class. Also in the class is a "model" girl student who is actually a slogan-shouting monster incapable of independent thinking. The problems of each are attributed to the chaos of the Cultural Revolution and the deception of the "gang of four." The story's dynamic thread is the teacher's effort to understand how these behavioral types emerged and how to transform them.

What will this group contribute to the four modernizations? Those who get a university education will have a chance to enter the technocratic elite; how creative they will be is another question. As for the majority, their apathy, low productivity, and sometime lawlessness are problems that the regime will have to take seriously if it has any hopes for the program's success.

The Swing Group in the Middle

This intermediate group combines several features of both the hard nosed thirty-year-olds and the naive teenagers. Like their elders, many urban youth in their mid-twenties are cynical because of the disillusioning experiences of the Cultural Revolution. But like the teenagers, they are young enough to have hopes for more education and for upward mobility. Many are very highly motivated and study foreign languages, technology, and philosophy on their own, even though their chances for further formal education are slim.

There are members of this generation who sincerely wish to make a contribution but find it difficult to do so. One such individual, a young factory worker hoping to show his superiors his knowledge of production, pleaded with me to obtain an American-made part for a particular machine. He knew that the part in question would last five times as long as the expensive Chinese-made one being used. When I asked why he did not make a recommendation to the factory technicians, he replied, "They'd never do it. They'd be too embarrassed to be shown up by an inferior and would also feel threatened. They can make life miserable for anyone who does that to them."*

Others in this swing group feel a broader frustration. As one twenty-six-year-old Shanghainese expressed it, "I'm eager to make some sort of contribution and do interesting work. But what I do requires just an animal's intelligence. My job is totally uninteresting, and I can complete in six hours what I'm supposed to do in a month. But there's no way for me to do more or switch jobs." Unchallenged by his job, he spends most of his time either gossiping about which male cadre is sleeping with which female employee, or trying to exchange cassette tapes out on the streets. "I like country and western music. Do you have any Dolly Parton tapes?"

Young people like him can be seen on the streets of many Chinese cities. They have adopted the accoutrements of a more individualistic life style--such as bell-bottom slacks and aviator sunglasses--and are tuning in to disco and rock and roll music. During the day they hawk the latest cassette tapes from Hong Kong and hang around tourists. At night they hold dance parties in their homes. In many ways the government is encouraging this trend. It has allowed domestic and foreign consumer

---

*Chinese factory technicians trained after the beginning of the Cultural Revolution often got no more than vocational training, and are now under pressure to improve their skills or else lose their jobs.

Young Chinese men spending their day off in a park outside Nanjing. (Picture by Jonathan Daen)

American tourists are the object of attention in the south China town of Foshan.

goods to be advertised in department store windows and on billboards formerly reserved for political slogans, and has increased the production and imports of such goods.

Because this swing group is both a resource and a liability for the four modernizations, the government is trying to win its support. The members of this generation received a stronger basic education and moral training than the teenagers, but are as astute at protesting as the Red Guards. They are not yet a lost generation, but the government's performance will dictate their loyalty. Unless they receive tangible rewards soon, they are unlikely to exert new effort.

There are two other categories of youth, one very large and the other apparently very small, whose voices are less audible. Their situation and attitudes can only be surmised.

The great majority of Chinese youth--around 75 percent in fact--live in the countryside and have little expectation of leaving their native place and the rigors of agricultural work. Because rural education is inferior to that in the cities, their passing the university entrance examination is unlikely. Many rural young people enlist in the People's Liberation Army as a way to get out. But they tend to be sent back to their villages upon demobilization, since the government is finding it hard enough to create jobs for urban youth, to say nothing of their country cousins.

The appeal of an urban job for peasant youth lies in the method of payment. Peasants' incomes are based on both individual effort and the total output of their production team. Urban workers, on the other hand, receive a fixed salary (though some bonuses have been instituted). Conversations with peasant youths--as well as city youths who had worked in the countryside and knowledgeable cadres--confirmed that most peasants would prefer any job with a guaranteed fixed wage and the welfare benefits that went along with it. But the best they can probably hope for is a rising standard of living, which the regime has tried to stimulate by increasing procurement prices of many agricultural goods and allowing more private production and marketing. The growth of rural industries that service agriculture will also make a difference. Whether peasant dissatisfaction will express itself politically, and with what effect, is difficult to say.

The other, much smaller group is the idealists, young people who have a spirit of "serving the people" either in the countryside or through a contribution to industrial or scientific modernization. Their number is difficult to estimate, and the odds against maintaining their sense of commitment are formidable.

A poignant example of this group is a young Shanghai girl who wrote an essay which a newspaper published at the suggestion of her teacher. She wrote of the difficulty of acting on her ideals in a spiritual void, where only a few individuals worked selflessly for communism. All she saw was hypocrisy, lies, self-indulgence, and a total absence of idealism. There were no realistic role models for her to follow, for everyone shouted slogans but refused to take the official ideals seriously. The newspaper ran a series of responses from readers. Most did not try to deny the crisis of confidence and the alienation of youth, but still urged the girl--unrealistically it seemed--to maintain her ideals.

THE CHINESE DIMENSION OF THE YOUTH PROBLEM

Many of the problems discussed above, especially unemployment and overpopulation, exist in most other developing countries. But there are social and political factors in China that introduce a unique dimension to the youth crisis.

Peasant Bureaucratism

Many of the cadres in charge of schools, factories, and other institutions were peasants who joined the Party as soldiers during the pre-1949 revolutionary period. They have the peasant's strong mistrust of intellectuals, and an endless succession of political campaigns and purges has left them reluctant to make any creative innovations. And many were just recently rehabilitated after ten or twenty years of disgrace, and are only concerned with enjoying the privileges of office and not jeopardizing their positions.

A college-educated woman in her late twenties described the situation in the south China defense plant where she works as a technician:

> The technical and scientific personnel in our factory are still stifled by the heavy-handed leadership of incompetent and unknowledgeable cadres sent in from the outside by the Party. Two people from our plant went to West Germany to study. They returned very eager to put into practice what they had learned, but they got depressed soon enough. There's no way you can perform at full capacity. It's best not to have an education. You think too much and realize too much, but are helpless to do anything about it.

A thirty-two-year-old worker in a sewing machine plant painted a bleak picture:

> The workers want a good place to work but now they feel it's a lost cause. The management is a mess.

There is a tremendous gap between labor and management. Some of the cadres are functionally illiterate and basically incompetent. All they have going for them are credentials as old revolutionaries. They have no overall strategy but operate defensively in trying to solve problems as they occur. I doubt if they even understand the policies sent from the center or could act on them if they did. In study sessions no one dares criticize them as you know they would find some way to nail you later.

Workers don't think in terms of an abstract "system." What matters to them is having enough to eat and wear, a television, a radio, and a sewing machine. They know and care little about Marxism-Leninism. There's a major cleavage between old and young workers. The old ones knew what life was like before Liberation, but it's useless to keep using this to sell the present setup to young people. You've got to look ahead and show them something tangible to work for.

Centralized Career Management

More than most countries, the government in China tries to regulate the flow of young people into employment and advanced education according to economic conditions and the prevailing political criteria. But this centralized "solution" to the unemployment problem has had a number of side effects:

--The approximately twelve million urban youth who went to the countryside (sometimes voluntarily, sometimes not) have refused to accept their fate quietly. Those remaining "down on the farm" have sometimes refused to work, disrupting production, and are generally regarded by peasants as a burden. Those who returned to the city illegally have lived an underground existence and disrupted social order.

--Urban high school students' anticipation of assignment to a life in the countryside contributed to lack of discipline in schools and crime outside them.

--Those lucky enough to get city jobs have very little say in their assignment, contributing to low productivity and disaffection in the workplace.

--Because university admissions in the 1970s were based on political loyalty, there is now a generation of poorly trained professionals in all fields.

The Absence of Genuine Role Models

Socialization by role modeling was a hallmark of traditional Chinese civilization (the statesman ruled as much by moral example as by active governance) and the Chinese Communist Party has acted within this tradition. Model workers, peasants, soldiers, and political figures have been and continue to be held up for national emulation. Local cadres were to serve as proximate examples of political rectitude.

But today, the socializing effect of models is now next to nil. Because contending leadership factions used official models as political weapons, cynicism about models is part and parcel of cynicism about politics in general. Local officials have been infected by corruption and special privilege, and their prestige has declined accordingly.

A story which appeared in Shanghai newspapers in September 1979 provides a dramatic example of the low esteem in which officialdom is held. It concerns a youth in his twenties, the son of a worker. He had been sent to a state farm for his obligatory stint as a peasant. Back in the city for Chinese New Year's vacation, he got a ticket to Much Ado About Nothing, the hottest show in town, by intimating that his father was a bigshot. One thing led to another, and, during a sixty-seven-day spree, prominent individuals offered him cars, women, watches, and living quarters as an investment in return for favors from his "father." The youth's deception was eventually discovered and he received a prison term. But he became an instant folk hero for exposing official hypocrisy.

Three local playwrights picked up the case and wrote a devastating satire, What If I Were Real?, that revealed the young man's true offense as far as the system was concerned. If he had actually been the son of a bigshot, the authors concluded, he never would have been arrested. His crime was that he was fake, only the son of a worker, a member of the supposed ruling class. The play whipped up a storm of controversy and was quickly banned.

THE GOVERNMENT'S RESPONSE AND PROSPECTS FOR THE FUTURE

With rare candor, the authorities have publicly acknowledged both the existence and scale of the youth problem. They have taken steps to rectify specific problems and are appealing to young people in a very different way from before. Whether this approach will succeed is far from certain, for it must be implemented by local officials whom youth often hold in disrespect, and whose careers and power are the most threatened by reform. It is certain, however, that progress in economic development depends on somehow stimulating the commitment of this large segment of the population.

To solve specific aspects of the youth problem, the government is:

— providing more opportunities for continuing education, through factory-run schools, television schools, correspondence courses, and allowing students who can afford tuition to enter university.
— improving career prospects for urban youth by cutting back the rustication program, giving high school graduates more say in their job assignments, permitting job switching, and allowing the formation of small-scale private enterprises.
— expanding political participation in the workplace through election of cadres by the workers, more promotions for young people, and greater power for professionally competent technicians. Incompetent or corrupt officials are to be replaced or punished.
— addressing the crisis of faith by discussing youth problems frankly and realistically in the media and popular literature, and offering more realistic role models.
— increasing construction of urban housing so that young couples will be able to live on their own rather than share cramped quarters with other family members.

More generally, the regime is deemphasizing the mass mobilization techniques of previous eras. To young people who say, "We can't be mobilized anymore," the Party now says, "The future is yours. Take your destiny in your own hands." Instead of mobilization, the Party is stimulating individual initiative through material, financial, educational, and political incentives.

In spite of these experiments, many urban young people are deeply skeptical about the possibility of fundamental and widespread change. They know that implementing these new policies is the responsiblity of middle- and lower-level bureaucrats, the very people they regard as the crux of China's problems. Confirming their suspicions, the Chinese media frequently criticize bureaucratic inaction and obstruction, and attack cadres' "special privileges." Although newspapers also cite examples of local leaders who have relinquished power and perquisites, young people tend to regard these as the exceptions that prove the rule.

What about the future? Young people in China's cities, on whom the modernization drive depends, must be convinced that individual intiative really will be encouraged and rewarded, that they will in fact have some control over their own destiny, and not be punished for sticking their necks out. Manipulated by slogans in the past, they will need more than rhetoric to dissolve their apathy and cynicism and to elicit commitment. For now, the obstacles are formidable.

6
Chinese Families and the Four Modernizations

Deborah Davis-Friedmann

INTRODUCTION

Since 1978 the Chinese Communist Party (CCP) has urged the people of China to "work confidently, devotedly, and with one mind for the realization of the splendid cause of the four modernizations." Citizens are repeatedly reminded that China's future depends on their willingness to sacrifice for the good of the nation. Yet the nation and the Party do not have a monopoly on the loyalties of the citizenry. Individuals also owe allegiance to their local community, to their friends, and, most importantly, to their families. Today there are 200 million households in China, and for most people family loyalties transcend all others.

What then is the impact of Chinese families on the current drive to realize the four modernizations? Do family loyalties reinforce government policies? Or do they present conflicting demands? Furthermore, how important can family life really be, three decades after the establishment of a socialist state?

Before answering these questions, it is necessary to define the word "family" and emphasize the critical differences between urban and rural households. In China, as elsewhere, the meaning of the word family varies by context. In ordinary speech, it may indicate a small household of wife, husband, and their unmarried children. Or it may refer to all living blood relations that recognize one another as kinfolk. In other circumstances, it is used to identify an individual's ancestors. The first two definitions are important for the discussion at hand, and in both these forms Chinese families play a critical role in the current drive for rapid economic growth and political stability.

Households in China are a basic unit of consumption and a primary locus of savings. They also fulfill key welfare functions: providing daily care of small children and the disabled. Defined as kinship, the families

67

have a smaller, but still significant role. Thirty years after the Communist victory, <u>kinship ties are strong</u> and many people give priority to family obligations.

Eight hundred million people live in the Chinese countryside. The land is densely populated, but the population is not concentrated into large settlements. Instead, most people live in small villages of fewer than three thousand inhabitants. <u>In some villages all the men share a single surname and recognize one common ancestor</u>. In others, as few as five or six family lines account for 90 percent of the community members. Thus in rural China <u>extended families are strong</u> and dominate many aspects of village life. In contrast, urban communities are large and impersonal. In the cities extended families are weak and even the household does not have the same emotional primacy as it does in the countryside. A review of the situation of Chinese families in 1949 and of their development under CCP rule explains how these differences between rural and urban family life directly affect the fate of the four modernizations.

FAMILY LIFE IN 1949: CRISIS

In 1949 families throughout China were under siege. If the Chinese Communists had in fact intended to destroy the multigeneration Confucian household as is sometimes alleged, their task would have been easy. Much of the destruction was already complete.

After more than a decade of warfare, flood, and famine, many rural households were small and unstable. In the countryside the most common household had four members and the poorest units had three. Diets were poor and public health measures inadequate. High infant mortality rates kept life expectancy at birth below forty years of age. Repeated conscription, frequent crop failure, and ineffective protection against infectious diseases threatened those family members who survived the rigors of childhood. As a result, few rural residents could plan on a peaceful old age surrounded by a spouse, married children, and several grandchildren. On the contrary, in most families at least one generation of the three would be missing or incomplete, and, for the vast majority, kinship resources were meager and family life was impoverished.

In the cities family life had also degenerated. Households were small and membership varied to accommodate frequent changes in employment. Among the working class, moreover, it was common for teenagers of both sexes to work outside the home before marriage. Untimely death, chronic illness, and unstable employment forced many young men and women to assume significant financial responsibilities, reversing the traditional authority of the old over the young and of men over women.

A sustained ideological attack against Confucian ideals of family authority further weakened the urban family structure. As first articulated by young intellectuals at the turn of the century, the critique focused on the authoritarian rule of family patriarchs and the subordination of women through the traditional practices of foot binding, child betrothal, and concubinage. By 1949, dissatisfaction with these practices was not limited to a handful of "progressive" intellectuals, and the ideals of monogamous love matches and democratic family relations had begun to filter down to young workers. On the eve of the CCP victory, therefore, the reality of urban family life rarely conformed to traditional expectations, and even the ideals of the old order had lost much of their validity.

FAMILIES UNDER THE CCP

Between 1949 and 1959 the CCP transformed the Chinese economy. Family farms, family businesses, and family-owned industries were among the first of the old institutions to disappear. Within a decade virtually all adult workers became employees of the state or of agricultural collectives. Rural and urban women entered the full-time work force in unprecedented numbers. Households were no longer important centers of production, and the government assumed much of the responsibility of training the next generation of workers and placing them in jobs.

Even before the Communist leaders had completed the economic reorganization of family life, they launched a frontal assault on traditional family structures. From 1950 to 1952 the CCP systematically enforced a Marriage Reform Law that proscribed concubinage, polygamy, and child betrothal. Within a decade marriage relations stood on new legal foundations. However, these fundamental changes in property rights and marriage practices, applicable to families throughout China, affected urban families differently than they did those in rural areas. In the cities the fragmented family life created by a combination of warfare and industrialization persisted. Peace and prosperity after 1949 restored order and increased the sense of security, but families did not gain in power and influence in relation to other economic and political organizations.

In the countryside, however, the family staged a remarkable comeback. Household size increased. Fathers and sons invested heavily in their jointly owned houses. Villagers were increasingly linked to one another by the mutual obligations of kinship, and families reemerged as the basic social institutions of rural life.

RURAL FAMILIES AFTER 1949

The revival of rural families under socialism can be attributed to four <u>elements of CCP economic development</u> policy. Their effect has been to stabilize, indeed enhance, the social role of families and reinforce certain traditional ideals.

I. The Household's Economic Responsibilities

The reorganization of the rural economy after 1949 proceeded in several phases, and each helped to shape the economic responsibility of the family. The land reform campaign of 1950-52 eliminated the right to be a landlord and redistributed 44 percent of arable land to the landless and land-poor. The drive for rural collectivization in 1956-57 eliminated the right of individuals to own, buy, or sell farm land, and established an entirely new form of <u>collective wage</u>s. All land became collective property, and wages for work done in the collectively owned fields reflected differences in only the quality and quantity of labor. Earlier efforts to recompense individuals who had contributed better quality land, draft animals, or tools was dropped, and a new system of "<u>workpoints</u>" became the sole criterion for distributing the collective harvest. In less than a decade the CCP completed the "socialist transformation" of agriculture.

The break from the past was rapid and radical. Yet in one dimension there was important continuity. As before 1949 the family remained a basic unit of responsibility in many legal and financial transactions. For example, during land reform the CCP deeded new land to families, and household size determined the size of the parcel. After collectives were established and the shift to the workpoint wage system accomplished, <u>the family continued to be the basic accounting unit for distributing income</u>. Thus even though workpoints assigned were based on the value of labor completed by an individual, the accounts were kept according to households. After the value of each workpoint was determined by the size of the final collective harvest, the cash and grain payments went to the household head, not the individual worker.

In addition to their responsibility in allocating income, families are also important as <u>independent units of production</u>. Since 1960 approximately 5 percent of arable land has been distributed to individual households in the form of "private plots." Although still owned collectively, this land is farmed by individual families and so retains a definite private character. Chinese peasants derive 25 to 30 percent of their annual income from these small plots. In some areas the percentage can exceed 50 percent. Therefore government planners as well as rural residents must recognize the large extent to which rural prosperity still depends on family endeavors.

2. Family Welfare Obligations

Traditionally, lineage organizations and family benevolent associations were responsible for social welfare in rural China. These institutional arms of the extended family disappeared after 1949, but immediate family members continued to be the first line of defense in times of crisis. The Marriage Law, as originally drafted in 1950 and as revised in 1980, holds adult children totally responsible for their indigent parents. Those who withhold financial support lose workpoints, and the grain or cash equivalent of these workpoints is transferred directly to their parents at harvest time.

Similarly, the general provisions for social welfare protection, in effect since 1956, reinforce traditional norms of familial responsibility. Only individuals who have lost all ability to work and are totally bereft of responsible kin may receive financial support from collective welfare funds. In most villages, the category "responsible kin" is defined to mean all sons and grandsons. In some cases it even extends to daughters, granddaughters, nieces, and nephews.

The consequences of post-1949 rural welfare policy are twofold. On the one hand, villagers continue to live in a world where mutual obligations and the norm of reciprocity permeate every phase of life. On the other, the government cannot make a frontal assault on kinship ties without risking a breakdown in the rural welfare system.

3. Restrictions on Migration

Before 1949 rural Chinese in trouble, or those with great ambition, could leave their families and begin a new life in another location. Migration out of the villages was frequent and the rural population was highly mobile. At the time of land reform CCP leaders optimistically believed that prosperity in the countryside would reduce these high levels of wartime migration, and took few steps to curb freedom of movement. The attraction of the cities, however, was irresistible to rural laborers. They flooded urban job markets and, whenever possible, moved their families with them.

In response to the upsurge of the urban population, the Chinese government severely restricted migration and eliminated the right of freedom of movement. New laws implemented in 1955 required all citizens to register one location as their permanent place of residence, and to secure the approval of the local public security office for any change of address. The only legal justification for relocation was an official job change. The exodus from the villages came to an abrupt halt, and choice of residence became a public, not private, decision. For agricultural laborers with little job mobility, these restrictions guaranteed that most adult sons would stay within the small communities of their parents, and that the rural population would become increasingly immobile.

4. Family Planning Policies

In the first decade of CCP rule, the government took no effective steps to control the number of births in rural areas. On the contrary, through 1958 all advocates of population control were attacked as anti-socialist Malthusians. Only in 1972 did the government make the first, sustained effort to enforce a strong family planning program in the countryside. Rural residents who had been socialized to equate large families with prosperity reacted as one would expect. Between 1950 and 1957 there were 167 million births in China, and between 1962 and 1971 another 267 million. At least 80 percent of these children were born to rural parents.

The consequences of high birth rates and restricted migration for rural family life were obvious. A village that had one thousand inhabitants in 1950 grew to two thousand by 1980, with virtually every new resident related by blood to one of the original thousand. Repeated in a million hamlets and villages, this pattern of population growth greatly intensified the importance and strength of family loyalties.

URBAN FAMILIES AFTER 1949

The development of urban families after 1949 was distinct from that of rural families. When, in the early 1950s, the CCP redesigned the urban economy, the work force was already highly individuated. The place of work was separated from the place of residence, and single workers, not family groups, were the basic work unit. Though the nationalization of industry and commerce radically reorganized the urban economy, it did not dramatically alter the position of the family vis-a-vis the workplace. Instead the socialization of the urban economy completed a process of separation of family and work already well established prior to 1949.

It would be inaccurate, however, to equate the decline of family-based production with the disintegration of the urban family. Urban households perform key social welfare functions, thus reducing government expenditures. As in the countryside, urban residents are required by law to support indigent parents if necessary, and welfare benefits are restricted to those totally bereft of kin. The majority of preschoolers are raised in their homes, and even the severely disabled remain in the daily care of their relatives at no cost to the state.

The urban family alsos play certain limited economic roles. As in the countryside, the household is a basic unit of consumption and distribution. Working members who live together pool their wages and often save jointly. Multigeneration households are common. Unmarried adults rarely establish independent residences, but instead live with parents sharing the family's supplies and furnishings. Such arrangements reduce demand for consumer items and permit the government to maximize investment in production.

The government restrictions that keep young rural men in the villages of their parents likewise contribute to the stability of urban family life. Even when a family member is transferred to a job in a distant province and remains there for several years, the official residence may remain unchanged and the individual may maintain a strong identification with the original household.

The impact of strong family ties in cities is not as great as in the villages, however. Extended families rarely live contiguously, and kinship ties do not permeate everyday life as they do in the countryside. When a rural resident sits at the doorstep of his home, he sees the community before him as the village of his family. The urban resident's family occupies a private space distinct from the public world of work and neighborhood. Emotional ties between urban relatives may be intense, but they can also be restricted to a limited sphere.

A household in the industrial city of Dalian. The older man is retired from the factory that provides the house. He, his wife, his daughter and son-in-law (neither of whom work in that factory), and his grandchild live together, thus reducing the demand for housing, consumer goods, and child care.

Since 1949 urban households and kinship networks have remained stable, and the government continues to demand high levels of mutual responsibility in social welfare matters. But in contrast to the situation in rural areas, municipal governments usually deal directly with individuals and do not need to work through households or make allowances for the economic and social influence of the extended family.

THE FAMILY AND THE FOUR MODERNIZATIONS

In light of the disparities between rural and urban families, can one identify any shared role that they play in the four modernizations? Surprisingly, the answer is yes. In the short term, both urban and rural families facilitate the drive for rapid economic growth and political stability.

Multigeneration households with several wage earners generate savings. The common practice of pooling individual incomes into one household budget mutes some of the resentment lower-income groups feel over income inequalities, thereby reducing pressure on the government to raise wages. Because the family absorbs many welfare functions, the public responsibilty for providing these services is less and the government can maximize its surplus for capital investment.

Strong family loyalties also contribute to political stability. In raising children, most Chinese families reward loyalty to the family group and penalize individualistic behavior that undermines reciprocity and mutual obligation. This type of family training reinforces the norms of obedience to superiors and loyalty to the group in other social situations.

Families do not provide unmitigated support for the four modernizations, however, for they may pose obstacles particularly in the long term. The most severe problems result from their age structure. Because of the large number of children born between 1950 and 1972, Chinese families in both rural and urban areas have a high ratio of consumers to producers.

This high dependency ratio places a severe strain on educational and employment resources. Between 1980 and 1990, about 22 million young people will enter the job market each year. Even if per capita expenditures remain constant, the cost of educating and employing these 220 million will be a drain on the government's budget. Yet educational resources are already inadequate to meet even current demands. Rural junior high schools cannot accommodate all the primary school graduates, and only 4 percent of all senior high graduates go on to university. Were the quality of education and job training to be improved, as modernization would seem to demand, the relative and absolute costs would increase significantly.

Guaranteeing permanent jobs for these young people is an even more serious obstacle. The problem is a latent one in the rural areas because the work force can still absorb additional manual laborers. In the cities, unemployment and underemployment cannot be so easily disguised. In the past two years approximately 50 percent of new high school graduates failed to receive long-term job assignments, but instead were assigned to temporary jobs in the service sector or to seasonal work.

This solution reduced the overall unemployment rate but created other problems. Young people perceive these jobs as a dead end, and accept them only because they are better than the alternative of agricultural work. The pay is too low to permit young workers to support independent households, and many, anxious to marry and begin their own families, are frustrated. This dissatisfied population of urban youth is large and highly visible. The size and urgency of their potential demands--for consumer goods and social services--continually serve to remind the leaders that their margin for error is narrow and that economic growth must be rapid and sustained.

In contrast to these material constraints, strong kinship loyalties pose an ideological obstacle to the success of the four modernizations. Early socialization at home does encourage a group orientation and obedience to authority, facilitating the current leadership's objectives. But the specific content of family loyalty may create a dilemma for the Party. In their homes children learn that their family is more important than any other group to which they belong. Nonfamily relationships are temporary; those of blood are permanent.

These family loyalties are of greatest consequence in the countryside, where villagers must rely on their kinfolk in good times and in bad. When family allegiances conflict with strictures imposed by the CCP and the government, the former take precedence and call into question the authority of leaders from outside the village to direct radical political or economic changes.

In the cities, where the household is not a fundamental economic unit and kinship ties are weaker, particularistic family loyalties do not seriously affect government priorities and policy implementation. Nevertheless, recent charges of nepotism and "entry through the back door" reflect the corrupting potential of family loyalties even in the most modern urban sector. Thus in both rural and urban China, it is possible that family solidarity can weaken the efficient administration and rational planning indispensable to the success of the four modernizations.

THE IMMEDIATE FUTURE

In 1980 and 1981 the government proposed two new

policies which directly addressed the future role of the Chinese family. The first advocated a one-child family as the ideal for the next thirty years. The second gave households more autonomy in relation to the collective in agricultural production.

In neither case has there been enough time to assess the long-range effects of these measures. The consequences of the birth control measures on family size, household composition, and the quality of parent-child relations will not be clear for at least one generation. The reorganization of agricultural work is an experiment limited to 20 percent of rural households. Even were this experiment expanded to the majority of villagers, we would need at least a decade to identify its long-term impact on families. Nevertheless, both these policies bring into sharp relief the relationship of families to the modernization effort.

The urgency of the birth control campaign is a clear indication of the seriousness of the population crisis. The rate of population increase threatens to nullify all the real economic gains made since 1949. Unless families reduce their size, it is feared, the promise of a dramatically improved standard of living will never be realized and the CCP will lose popular support.

The decision to increase the responsibilities of individual households in agricultural collectives is testimony to the fundamental role of the household in the Chinese economy. When national leaders appeal to the family to increase production they are publicly stating that households control essential reserves that are otherwise inaccessible through special efforts of production teams or individual workers. In recognizing the rural household as an especially efficient unit of production, the leadership acknowledges the centrality of families to the future growth of the Chinese economy.

Thirty years after the establishment of a socialist state, Chinese families play a crucial role in national development programs. In the countryside their economic contribution is particularly self-evident, and failure to deal wisely with the needs and strengths of rural households and kinship links can threaten national prosperity. In providing for the needs of the financially dependent, both urban and rural families fulfill a welfare function that directly supports government priorities.

Strong family loyalties, however, have an ambiguous effect. To the extent that they subordinate individual interests to those of large social units, families tend to encourage stability, order, and obedience. However, to the extent that family loyalties are primary, or even exclusive, they can engender nepotism, localism, and the ascendancy of private over public concerns.

In spite of this dual potential, one observation on the role of the family stands before all others. In

1981, after more than a generation of "socialist transformation," the Chinese Communists have not eradicated the importance of family life, and families in their several forms continue to shape the basic parameters in which political and economic experiments either succeed or fail.

7
US–China Relations in 1980

John Bryan Starr

INTRODUCTION

As President Reagan's administration took office, it faced two difficult and interrelated issues concerning US policy toward China. One--relations with Taiwan--was raised by the president himself during the campaign. The other--whether to continue a "tilt" toward China, especially in the military sphere--is a legacy of the previous administration. How the first issue is handled will determine China's approach to the second.
During 1980 the United States completed the normalization of relations with the People's Republic of China, and, in the process, ended the policy of "evenhanded" treatment of China and the Soviet Union. Moscow accelerated this shift in US policy, which began in mid-1979, by its invasion of Afghanistan. The resulting US ties with China are closer than those with any other socialist country, though falling short of an alliance. But the relationship is still tentative: the new administration will have to define and elaborate it more precisely.
Ronald Reagan's own campaign statements have complicated this task. By suggesting that the US deal with Taiwan on more than an "unofficial" basis, he created concern in China that the US might renege on promises made at the time of normalization. The new administration backed away from that proposal once in office. In March 1981 Secretary of State Haig called US-China relations "a strategic reality and . . . imperative . . . of overriding importance," and pledged that the US would abide by both the normalization communique and the Taiwan Relations Act.* Despite of these assurances, Beijing will be waiting for Washington to clarify its position on the Taiwan issue before it agrees to expanded economic and security relations.

---

*Appendix B contains documents on US-PRC relations.

1980: COMPLETING NORMALIZATION, ENDING EVENHANDEDNESS

Political Developments

Prior to mid-1979 the Carter administration fashioned relations with China in accordance with the principle of "evenhandedness" toward Beijing and Moscow. This principle dictated that, in general, the US should extend to China those favors extended to the Soviet Union, and vice versa.* Some administration officials began questioning this approach as early as 1977. Zbigniew Brzezinski, the president's national security advisor, was widely assumed to favor an anti-Soviet, pro-Chinese approach, while Cyrus Vance, then secretary of state, was assumed to be a champion of evenhandedness. The pro-China tilt became public in August 1979 during Vice President Mondale's visit to China, when, in a speech at Beijing University, he spoke of the "mutual security interests" shared by the US and the PRC.

With the Soviet invasion of Afghanistan in December 1979, Washington took a series of steps that effectively ended the policy of evenhandedness. First, President Carter made two decisions in January 1980 regarding the transfer of technical equipment to China. One allowed China greater access to American dual-use (military as well as civilian) technology. The other permitted American firms to export nonlethal military equipment to China on a case-by-case basis. Neither of these provisions applied to the Soviet Union.

Two days after these decisions were made, Defense Secretary Harold Brown arrived in Beijing, the first high-level military contact between the US and China in more than thirty years. The trip, initially intended as the beginning of a dialogue between the defense establishments of the two countries, had been arranged early in the fall of 1979. At that time American assistance to the Chinese military seemed out of the question: a Defense Department study suggested that it would cost between forty-one and sixty-three billion dollars to give China a "confident capability" to defend itself against a Soviet conventional attack. But the Soviets' Afghan adventure added urgency to the visit, and it was used to create the impression of rapidly developing military cooperation and to explore joint means of encouraging or supporting Afghan resistance groups.

Brown's Chinese hosts seemed to be both surprised and somewhat bemused by the eagerness with which he

---

*The Kremlin accepted full diplomatic normalization between the US and China on the grounds that it corrected what had been, in effect, an imbalance in US-Soviet and US-China relations.

US Secretary of Defense Harold Brown is greeted in Beijing by PRC Vice Premier Geng Biao. (Wide World Photos)

---

presented his suit. On the one hand they were clearly pleased to hear the secretary of defense describe Soviet actions in the same terms they themselves had used for many months. On the other hand, they appeared not to have prepared concrete suggestions of countermeasures.

During the course of the Brown visit, the language used by American officials to define the US-PRC relationship changed substantially. Prior to Brown's departure, Defense Department officials said that US policy still called for a "balanced" treatment of the Soviet Union and China. While in China, those accompanying Brown took a different line, suggesting that the evenhanded approach had become "frayed," and that there was no point in treating Moscow and Beijing with an even hand "since they behave so differently toward us." Brown himself called for "parallel" or "complementary" actions where US-PRC interests coincided, and suggested that it was time to move from "passive to more active forms of security cooperation."

The visit had several significant results, both concrete and symbolic. To impress Moscow, Secretary Brown emphasized that "the fact of the visit is its own central feature"; the Chinese suggested ways they were prepared to assist in thwarting Soviet aggression in Afghanistan. To continue the discussion of military affairs, Vice

Premier Geng Biao, secretary-general of the Chinese Communist Party's Military Commission, accepted an invitation to visit the US, but the Chinese rejected the opening of a hot line between the two capitals. In terms of concrete assistance, the US agreed to make available to the Chinese equipment for monitoring data on crops and geological deposits from the Landsat D satellite to be launched early in 1981. Apparently, China did not ask to purchase US arms, and Brown indicated publicly that massive military purchases of any kind were unlikely. A lack of foreign exchange, the problems of assimilation with existing equipment, and the negative lessons regarding military dependency drawn from their experience in the 1950s all had a bearing on the Chinese decision.

Washington took another step away from evenhandedness in late May 1980 when Geng Biao visited the US, ahead of schedule. While Geng was in Washington, the Pentagon announced a further easing of US export restrictions on military-related equipment for China. During the visit, Secretary Brown called for "step-by-step strengthening of ties between our two defense establishments as an integral part of our effort to normalize all facets of our relationship."

On June 4, immediately following Geng's visit (and following Cyrus Vance's resignation), Richard Holbrooke, assistant secretary of state for East Asia and the Pacific, made the policy shift official. Speaking before the National Council for US-China Trade, he said that China was to be given preference over the Soviet Union and the policy of evenhandedness was to be abandoned. However, the US would continue to regard China as a "friend," not as an "ally."

The new relationship was explored further when President Carter met with Hua Guofeng, then China's premier, in Tokyo on the occasion of memorial services for deceased Japanese Premier Ohira on July 10. It was elaborated with much greater specificity by William Perry, under secretary of defense for research and engineering, when he visited Beijing in September 1980 to study China's ability to absorb American technology. During his visit, Perry announced that the US government had cleared more than 400 export licenses covering equipment for China ranging from trucks and transport planes through helicopters, flight simulation equipment, and aerial cameras, to long-range radar installations. Also under consideration was the sale of a geophysical data computer with potential military application. For their part, the Chinese agreed to make rare metals of military relevance available for sale to the US.

The Carter administration's initiatives provoked reactions from both domestic critics and the Soviet Union. Representative Lester Wolff (D-N.Y.), then chairman of the House Subcommittee on East Asia and the

Pacific, headed a delegation to Beijing shortly after Brown returned home in January. Following his own return, Wolff asserted that the administration was moving toward a military alliance with China without having investigated China's needs and what the US might expect in return. Wolff subsequently scheduled hearings on the subject, and some of those testifying argued strongly for a return to an evenhanded approach to relations with Moscow and Beijing.

Others took up the argument, noting that the US could not provide China with enough military help to truly enhance its security vis-a-vis the forty-five Soviet divisions on its northern border. Some observers were skeptical about "playing the China card" to influence Soviet-American relations. As Joseph Harsch of the Christian Science Monitor put it, "Any bridge player knows [that] a trump card can only be played once." Those who proposed that Washington should play a "Vietnam card" against the Soviet Union felt that a close US alignment with China would give Hanoi no incentive to end its exclusive reliance on Moscow.

Soviet reaction, as expressed in the official media, was subdued for the most part. But Soviet President Leonid Brezhnev, in a conversation with the French politician Jacques Chalban-Dalmas, vigorously denounced American moves toward a closer relationship with China, suggesting somewhat contemptuously that, in the event of a Soviet preemptive nuclear attack on China, the US would be both unwilling and unable to come to the assistance of its newfound Asian "ally." Such predictions did not stop China from joining the US boycott of the summer Olympic Games in Moscow. It also rejected out of hand a Soviet overture to reconvene negotiations (begun in September 1979) to restore normal relations between Moscow and Beijing.

To sum up, the Carter administration in its last eighteen months abandoned evenhandedness both rhetorically and in terms of stated policy. But Carter's successor, together with China's leaders, would have to decide how to translate into action the two countries' increasingly similar perceptions of the Soviet threat.

Economic Developments

Building on negotiations in 1979, US-China economic relations were normalized in 1980. Most importantly, Congress approved the Sino-American trade agreement in January, thereby granting China most-favored-nation treatment. In September the two countries signed agreements covering textile trade, maritime relations, and aviation relations. Total two-way trade increased in 1980 to almost five billion dollars, more than double the 1979 figure, four times the 1978 amount. The year also

US Treasury Secretary G. William Miller and PRC Vice Premier Bo Yibo at beginning of discussions of economic relations in September 1980. Chai Zemin, PRC ambassador to the US, and Leonard Woodcock, then US envoy to China, look on. While in Washington, Bo signed on China's behalf four agreements with the US. (Wide World Photos)

saw two major trade exhibitions: Chinese exhibitions were held in San Francisco, Chicago, and New York from September through December; and an American exhibition--among the largest ever sponsored by the Department of Commerce--was held in Beijing in November.

The textile agreement was the most complex of the four concluded. The PRC has tried to reduce its trade deficit with the United States by expanding exports, particularly textiles and clothing. In 1979 those commodities constituted half of PRC exports to the US; only Hong Kong, South Korea, Taiwan, and Japan shipped more textiles to the US. American textile producers lobbied strongly against allowing the PRC even greater access to the American market. China countered by noting that its textile exports were made primarily with imported American natural and synthetic fibers. Discussions continued, but not successfully enough to prevent a renewal of those quotas in May 1980. After eighteen months of negotiations and imposition of unilateral US quotas, a compromise agreement was eventually reached in the late summer.

The civil aviation agreement was delayed because the US wanted to open the China route to more than one airline. As finally signed, the agreement calls for an initial air route from New York to Beijing. A second route is to open at the end of a two-year period. The maritime agreement opened fifty-five American ports to

Chinese ships and twenty Chinese ports to American vessels.*
 More generally, China took new steps to expand its role in the world economy. Beijing elaborated the legal framework for the conduct of joint ventures and established special economic zones for international economic ventures in the southern provinces of Guangdong and Fujian. Foreign involvement in major development projects was sought. In March, for example, an American delegation from the Tennessee Valley Authority and the US Army Corps of Engineers signed an agreement to work with the Chinese on four major hydroelectric projects: two on the Red River, one on a tributary of the Yangzi River, and one on the Yangzi itself. The agreement provided for 25 American engineers to work on the projects in China and 100 Chinese engineers to study in the US. In April Beijing replaced Taiwan in the World Bank and the International Monetary Fund (IMF).#
 China's entry into the IMF raised questions among other developing nations regarding China's future share of Fund borrowing rights. A more basic question was the extent to which China would be able to take advantage of foreign credits at all, whether from international organizations, banks, or foreign governments (twenty-eight billion dollars was available from the latter two sources). Chinese leaders debated the wisdom of borrowing to finance economic development, particularly since China had yet to create the necessary infrastructure for many of these projects. With the revelation in early September that China's 1980 state budget would have a deficit of some eleven billion dollars, the government decided to delay or terminate a number of joint development projects, including a $250 million trade center

---

*A fourth agreement, signed at the same time as the economic agreements, covered consular affairs. It regulates consular duties and privileges and allows each country to open three more consulates. China, which has consulates in Houston and San Francisco, plans to open new ones in New York, Chicago, and Honolulu. The US has consulates in Guangzhou and Shanghai and intends to open offices in Shenyang, Wuhan, and Chengdu. Lack of reciprocity in the purchase of property is a continuing problem: the Chinese bought their third New York building in 1980 but have consistently blocked American attempts to purchase property in Beijing for housing and offices.

#Taiwan's loss was less economic than political. The island's economy did not suffer, for the Nationalists had not exercised their borrowing rights for some time. But the ouster did increase their sense of de jure isolation in the world community.

in Beijing. These decisions, which led some American corporations to lower their hopes for expanded involvement in China in the near term, only served to highlight continuing uncertainty about the possible and appropriate American role in PRC development, an issue that will be on the Reagan administration's China policy agenda.

Cultural Relations

Nineteen-eighty saw a proliferation of governmental and private exchanges in the fields of <u>culture</u>, <u>education</u>, and <u>research</u>. At the beginning of the year there were some 1,500 Chinese scholars and students studying in the US, one-third under private sponsorship and the rest with Chinese government support. By year's end that number had nearly quadrupled to about 6,000. The number of Americans studying in China under official or institution-to-institution arrangements increased from 300 to nearly 500 by year's end. In August the Chinese announced that 2.7 million people had visited China as tourists during the first six months of the year, including more than 60,000 Americans. Although few Chinese visited the US as tourists, Chinese delegations were visiting this country at a rate of 100 per month by early fall.

As exchanges multiplied, both sides had to come to grips with the question of reciprocity, both in terms of numbers and access. Clearly, the respective needs and interests of Chinese and American visiting scholars have been asymetrical from the outset. Beijing's <u>priorities for sending scholars abroad lie first in the natural and basic sciences</u>. Chinese scholars in the social sciences and humanities have thus found it more difficult to secure funds from their government to go abroad. While some American scientists find research in China useful for their own work, the majority of American scholars seeking access to China have been those with an interest in Chinese history, literature, politics, economics, or social issues. But these disciplines are only beginning a post-Cultural Revolution revival, and Chinese have found it difficult to accommodate American counterparts. This has been true not only for field work, but also for library or archival research.

The initial eagerness on the part of American colleges and universities to welcome Chinese students and scholars has gradually been tempered by a realization of the problems of funding and introducing Chinese to American student life. More broadly, many institutions have come to feel the need for a firmer American bargaining position on exchange relationships which would insure that the exchanges are in fact reciprocal. Without greater reciprocity, some believe the exchanges are not likely to endure.

On the Chinese side, the growing foreign presence has caused concern and has resulted in new regulations governing contacts between Chinese citizens and foreigners residing in China. Some steps were taken to discourage Chinese from making friends with members of the foreign community and even from making contact with them on other than official occasions. These regulations appeared to be enforced with varying degrees of thoroughness, however, particularly outside of Beijing. As a result, many American scholars and teachers have enjoyed good access to research materials and fruitful contacts with their students and colleagues.

Chinese ambivalence about closing the wide cultural gap between the two countries was also illustrated by the process involved in setting up an American film festival in China. Of twelve representative American films presented, the Chinese rejected all but two (Snow White and the Seven Dwarfs and The Black Stallion) as "inappropriate." In the end the Chinese agreed to include Shane, Singing in the Rain, and Guess Who's Coming to Dinner in the film festival. Meanwhile, the Chinese chose decidedly inferior films for separate distribution, apparently because of their low cost rather than their "appropriateness" or "representativeness." The continuing obstacles to cross-cultural understanding were again obvious.

THE TAIWAN QUESTION

The Reagan administration thus took office at a time when US-China relations have yet to be clearly defined strategically, fully realized economically, and genuinely reciprocal in the cultural sphere. Prior to deciding its direction in these areas, however, the new administration will have to confront the task of clarifying for itself, for the American public, and for Taipei and Beijing, its position regarding the "Taiwan issue" that Reagan revived during the course of the presidential campaign.

Reagan's position on Taiwan, articulated initially in May 1980 and subsequently reiterated and refined, focused on two issues: the status of US representation in Taiwan and the scope of US arms sales to Taiwan. The Taiwan Relations Act of 1979 stipulated that the relationship between Washington and Taipei was to be unofficial, conducted on each side through nongovernmental organizations staffed by foreign service personnel retired or on leave from government service. Reagan argued that the relationship should be an official one. He cited as a model the use of liaison offices for conducting relations between the US and the PRC prior to normalization.

The Chinese response was immediate and sharply worded. People's Daily denounced Reagan's position in an editorial on June 14 as a "futile attempt to turn back the clock." Following his nomination by the Republican party in August, Reagan sent his vice presidential running mate, George Bush, to Beijing to clarify the Republican position on Taiwan. Before departing, Bush expressed confidence that he would be able to clear the air based on his experience as head of the US Liaison Office in China in the mid-1970s. The Chinese bluntly described his trip as a failure. Moreover, the statement distributed to news media by the Reagan campaign following Bush's return served only to reinforce the impression that Reagan sought a change in the status of American relations with Taiwan.

Attempting to ward off the potential ill effects of Reagan's remarks, Senator Robert Byrd (D-W.Va.) told Chinese leaders during a visit to Beijing in July that there could be no "turning back of the clock," and that no future American president could avoid living up to the provisions of the Taiwan Relations Act, which could only be amended by congressional, not by executive action. Following the Bush visit, US Ambassabor Leonard Woodcock called an unprecedented press conference in Beijing to reinforce Byrd's argument.

In retrospect, several things seem clear. First, Reagan's comments were personally inspired by his long-standing admiration for Taiwan's leaders, their achievements, and their American supporters. Second, the Nationalists on Taiwan apparently did not prompt Reagan's proposal. While they undoubtedly wanted a better normalization deal, they seem basically satisfied with the mechanisms established to conduct "unofficial" relations with the US (the American Institute in Taiwan and its counterpart, the Coordination Council for North American Affairs). Third, the public airing of the question served to make explicit to the American public ambiguous aspects of the Taiwan Relations Act. Fourth, Reagan rubbed a sensitive PRC nerve by intimating that, if elected, he might treat US relations with Taiwan as official. The Carter administration's subsequent decision to grant diplomatic immunity to Taiwan's representatives in the US only deepened suspicions in Beijing, and this could complicate US-China relations in the period ahead.

US arms sales to Taiwan add another layer to PRC suspicion. Beijing reacted negatively to the announcement in January 1980 that the US planned to sell Taiwan $280 million in arms, though the Brown visit probably muted the initial Chinese response. But the Chinese press took up the question more fully and more critically in June, perhaps because of the news that Washington was permitting informal talks to go forward between representatives of the government of Taiwan and American manufacturers of "FX" fighter planes. At this point People's Daily asserted that the $800 million in orders that the

US filled in 1979 to honor "past commitments" and the $280 million in sales in 1980 were in clear violation of the Chinese position regarding the normalization agreement with the US, and could lead only to instability in the Taiwan Strait.*

Immediately after the American election, Chinese attitudes vacillated widely. Though the Taiwan issue had faded from public view in the US by November, many Chinese directly connected with US-China relations continued to express considerable concern. This subsided when Deng Xiaoping expressed conciliatory remarks about the new American president. Then, Ray Cline, a Georgetown University professor in the Reagan camp, made statements on a trip to Taiwan in December that aroused new fears in the PRC about the incoming administration's intentions. The PRC took heart from Secretary of State Haig's statement in March 1981 stressing the strategic basis of the relationship, and similar messages conveyed by former President Gerald Ford, who visited China the same month. But having raised expectations in Taiwan, kindled apprehension in Beijing, and created confusion among Americans, the Reagan team's task of clarifying its policy on relations with Taiwan is not over.

How would China react should Washington attempt to alter its relationship with Taiwan? The government's hands are not completely tied by domestic political considerations. A close and friendly relationship with Washington is, of course, of considerable advantage to China. Moreover, much of the brouhaha in China regarding Reagan's statements is the product of the Chinese government's own press treatment of the episode.

---

*As for the relationship between Taipei and Beijing, informal contacts expanded considerably during 1980. Taipei quietly retreated from total rejection of Beijing's proposals for various forms of contact and interaction. Consequently, sailors from the PRC were welcomed in Taiwan; scholars from Taiwan and the PRC attended conferences in Japan, Europe, and the US; and press coverage of conditions in the PRC and Taiwan was increased on both sides. While Taiwan continued to maintain an official ban on trade with the PRC, Beijing announced a series of regulations to encourage growth of that trade. Statistics released in Hong Kong in July indicated that two-way trade between Taiwan and the PRC through Hong Kong had reached a figure of $46 million for the first quarter of 1980--a 400% increase over the same period in 1979. The Chinese press persistently argued that Taiwan's economy was jeopardized by its dependence on oil imports, and suggested that the trade of manufactured goods from Taiwan for oil and other raw materials from the PRC would enhance the development of both economies.

Yet, it should be noted, there have been signs that the PRC's pro-American foreign policy is not universally popular among the Chinese people. For example, in a speech published in the official newspaper of the Communist Youth League in spring 1980, Zhang Guangdou, who studied in the US prior to 1949 and who is now vice president of the prestigious Qinghua University in Beijing, asserted that America's role in the world was one of continued imperialist aggression. He pointedly noted that the current warm relationship between Beijing and Washington should be understood as only a short-term tactical move on China's part, not as a permanent reordering of Chinese foreign policy priorities.

Although Zhang's remarks were subsequently dismissed as insignificant by Deng Xiaoping and others, it is highly likely that Zhang's views are not unique among Chinese intellectuals and government cadres. Such skepticism could well get a better hearing in Beijing were the new administration in Washington to pursue a policy toward Taiwan that was seen as inimical to the interests of the PRC. The credibility of the foreign policy of Deng and his colleagues could be called into question, thereby weakening the legitimacy of the current leadership. Thus the US government should not overestimate the degree of flexibility that the Chinese government can exercise on the Taiwan issue.

BEYOND THE TAIWAN ISSUE

Even if the Taiwan issue does not impede the continued development of broader US-China relations, the new administration must nevertheless clarify its policy toward China. The president and his advisers must decide how to build on the foundation laid by their predecessors while taking into account US relations with other powers in the Pacific basin.

In the strategic realm, the Reagan administration must decide the degree to which China and the US can and should effectively cooperate militarily. China is seen by some as a counterpoise against Soviet influence in Asia. While the size of the Chinese population and resource base is impressive, it is nonetheless clear that China is not now and will not be for some time a credible military makeweight against the militarily powerful and sophisticated Soviet presence in Asia. Thus the future utility of a "tilt" in China's direction in the triangular relationship between Moscow, Beijing, and Washington must be carefully considered.

In economic terms, the US business community must come to grips with the fact that the PRC is a less than perfect trading partner given its present level of development and policies for the future. While there is a Chinese interest in sophisticated American technology and a reciprocal American interest in Chinese raw materials, particularly oil, these interests are not likely to result in an especially high volume of trade. American corporations must be given a sober and realistic picture of the likely constraints in the development of US trade and investment in China, even with the removal of past official obstacles to commercial interaction.

In the cultural sphere, those responsible for governmental as well as for private exchange programs must address the question of reciprocity. Without a shared sense of benefit from these programs, there is a strong possibility that irritation and discord could arise.

****

Some of the conditions for dealing with these issues already exist. An official framework of relations has been established for the first time in thirty years. There appears to be broad public support and sound political and economic reasons on both sides for expanding the relationship. The final ingredient--political leadership--has yet to be fully measured.

Appendix A:
Biographical Sketches
of Members of the Politburo
of the Chinese Communist Party

(This appendix includes those individuals who were at least nominal Politburo members as of July 1, 1981. The Wade-Giles form of their names is given parenthetically at the beginning of each entry. PLA = People's Liberation Army.)

MEMBERS OF THE STANDING COMMITTEE

Hu Yaobang (Hu Yao-pang), Party Chairman and General Secretary

Hu Yaobang was born in 1915 in Mao's home province of Hunan. Early in his career he specialized in youth work, and participated in the Long March. After war broke out with Japan in 1937, he worked in the military's commissariat. In 1941 Hu became a subordinate of Deng Xiaoping, and the two have worked together ever since. From 1949 to 1952, years that Deng Xiaoping worked in Sichuan, Hu was a key official in the province's northern region.

Then in 1952 he returned to his original field, becoming head of the Communist Youth League. He entered the Central Committee in 1956, and generally spent the next decade in Beijing, except for a brief interlude in Shaanxi province in early 1965 as acting first Party secretary. During the Cultural Revolution, Hu was denounced as a follower of Liu Shaoqi, and had to undergo a period of "reeducation." In 1975, during Deng's short-lived return to power, Hu worked on science policy.

With Deng's rehabilitation in mid-1977, Hu began his climb to the top. Late that year he became director of the Party's organization department. At the third plenum of the Eleventh Central Committee in December 1978, he became a Politburo member, Party secretary-general, and third secretary of the Central Commission for Inspecting Discipline. At about this time, he moved from the Party

93

organization department to its propaganda department. At the February 1980 fifth plenum, Hu was elevated to the standing committee of the Politburo and was named to head of the newly reconstituted Party Secretariat, with the title of general secretary. (He is no longer director of the Party propaganda department.) The sixth plenum of the Central Committee in June 1981 confirmed rumors circulating since late 1980 that Hu had indeed replaced Hua Guofeng as Party chairman.

Ye Jianying (Yeh Chien-ying), Party Vice Chairman

Born in 1898, Ye was a major military figure during the revolution and a close collaborator of Zhou Enlai. He was on the Long March and served as chief-of-staff of the PLA in the late 1940s. After 1949 he served as mayor of Guangzhou and governor of his native Guangdong Province. With the reorganization of the PLA after the Korean War, Ye was named director of the PLA inspectorate and was elected to the Party's Military Commission. During the mid-1950s he was an outspoken advocate of military modernization. He was elected to the Politburo in January of 1967 and became a Party vice chairman in 1973. After the purge of Lin Biao in 1971, Ye was placed in charge of military affairs and was formally named minister of defense in 1975.

Since Mao's death in 1976, Ye has shed many of his responsibilities and played the role of Party elder. He was instrumental in the arrest of the "gang of four," and was a strong supporter of Hua Guofeng's becoming Party chairman. He has taken an interest in constitutional reform of both Party and state structures. In early 1978 he turned over the national defense portfolio to Xu Xiangqian but became chairman of the standing committee of the National People's Congress (equivalent to head of state).

In late September 1979, on the leadership's behalf, Ye delivered a major address marking the thirtieth anniversary of the founding of the People's Republic. In it he rejected Mao's definition of revisionism, thus eroding the ideological justification of the Cultural Revolution. However, Ye reportedly resisted the 1980 posthumous rehabilitation of Liu Shaoqi and the demotion of Hua Guofeng.

Deng Xiaoping (Teng Hsiao-p'ing), Party Vice Chairman

Born in Sichuan in 1904, Deng joined the Chinese Communist Party in 1924 while on a work-study program in France. A veteran of the Long March, he assumed important posts in the political commissariat in the Red Army, eventually becoming the political commissar of the Second Field Army under Liu Bocheng. After 1949 Deng served for three years in southwest China, but was transferred to Beijing in 1952, becoming a vice premier and serving briefly as minister of finance. In 1954 he became secretary-general of the Central Committee, where he was responsible for the day-to-day work of the Party. The following year he was elected to the Politburo, and in 1956 his title was changed to general secretary, reflecting an increase in his power.

Deng held both those positions until the Cultural Revolution and was considered, along with Mao, Zhou, and Liu Shaoqi, one of the most powerful men in China. During the Cultural Revolution he was accused of following "Liu Shaoqi's revisionist line" and was dismissed from office.

Deng was rehabilitated in April 1973 and resumed his vice premiership. He was returned to the Politburo in late 1973, and in early 1975 became a vice chairman of the Party and chief-of-staff of the military. He also took charge of the day-to-day work of the Party. Soon, however, his criticism of Cultural Revolution programs and his plans for China's economic development aroused the opposition of Mao's radical followers. In April 1976 they succeeded in having him purged for a second time. After Mao's death and considerable discussion within the Politburo, Deng was restored to his various posts at the third plenum of the Tenth Central Committee in July 1977. Gradually thereafter he achieved a preeminent political position by facilitating a nearly total reversal of the verdict on the Cultural Revolution, on its victims (including his former ally Liu Shaoqi), and on Mao himself.

Deng has been the prime mover in China's post-Mao "great leap outward." In the fall of 1978 he himself traveled to Japan to sign the Sino-Japanese Treaty of Peace and Friendship, and to Southeast Asia to shore up China's diplomatic position against Vietnam. The following January he came to the US to celebrate the normalization of relations.

As part of the transfer of power to younger leaders, Deng gave up his army chief-of-staff post in April 1980 and his vice premiership in September of the same year. With Hua Guofeng's resignation from his top Party posts in late 1980, Deng took over the duties of Party Military Commission chairman. His protege, Hu Yaobang, formally became Party chairman in June 1981, replacing Hua Guofeng.

Zhao Ziyang (Chao Tzu-yang), Party Vice Chairman and Premier of the State Council

Born in 1919 in Henan Province, Zhao is a veteran Party cadre with extensive experience in south China. Between 1951 and 1955 he was secretary-general of the

Party's south China bureau, responsible for Guangdong and Guangxi provinces. He then rose gradually in the Guangdong provincial Party apparatus, finally becoming first Party secretary in 1965.

Purged during the Cultural Revolution as a "revisionist," Zhao was rehabilitated in 1971 and sent to Inner Mongolia to serve on the provincial Party committee. By March 1972 he was back in Guangdong and was named first secretary in April 1974. In December 1975 he was transferred to Sichuan, China's most populous province, to become first Party secretary, chairman of the provincial revolutionary committee, and first political commissar of the Chengdu Military Region.

Since Deng Xiaoping's July 1977 rehabilitation, Zhao has rapidly gained political prominence. He made Sichuan a pacesetter in a number of policy areas, particularly economic management and population control. He was elected an alternate member of the Politburo at the Eleventh Party Congress (August 1977), a full member at the Central Committee's fourth plenum (September 1979), and a member of the standing committee at the fifth plenum (February 1980).

In early 1980, Zhao moved from the provinces to the center. Having relinquished his posts in Sichuan, he became a vice premier in April, and it was soon revealed that he had taken charge of the day-to-day work of the State Council, previously Deng Xiaoping's responsibility. He became premier in September 1980, replacing Hua Guofeng. Though his political standing may have suffered somewhat in late 1980 because the economic liberalization he advocated contributed to inflation, he was still named a Party vice chairman in June 1981.

Li Xiannian (Li Hsien-nien), Party Vice Chairman

Born in Hubei Province about 1905, Li was a commander in the Red Army before 1949 and a veteran of the Long March. In the early 1950s he was governor of his native province and held several other important positions in the central-south region. Li became finance minister in 1954, succeeding Deng Xiaoping. He was soon promoted to vice premier, with responsibility for all financial and trade matters. He entered the Politburo in September 1956.

Li was one of the few high-ranking economic planners to remain in office throughout the Cultural Revolution, and he became a Party vice chairman at the Eleventh Party Congress in August 1977. He was chiefly responsible for drafting the Ten-Year Plan unveiled in February 1978, which called for rapid growth of heavy industry and the importation of whole plants from abroad. Since early 1979 that policy has been attacked for neglecting the material needs of the Chinese people. In September 1980

Li gave up his vice premiership, and, late in the year, reportedly made a self-criticism of his economic leadership.

Chen Yun (Ch'en Yun), Party Vice Chairman

Chen was born around 1900 (some say 1905) in Jiangsu Province. He participated in part of the Long March, and spent time in Russia in the mid-1930s. In 1945 he was elected to the Politburo and made a member of its inner circle. With the founding of the PRC in 1949 he became one of four vice premiers, and worked closely with Zhou Enlai to rehabilitate the economy. He became a Party vice chairman in 1956.

In the debates surrounding the Great Leap Forward, which Mao initiated in the late 1950s, Chen continually called for measured, steady, and systematic growth, to be stimulated by material incentives rather than mass mobilization. Thus in the early 1960s he played a significant role in bringing the economy out of its post-Leap depression. But because of Mao's growing fears that such pragmatism was leading China down the road of revisionsim, Chen was politically inactive from 1962 until Mao's demise and the purge of the "gang of four" in 1976. (Formally, Chen lost his major positions during the 1966-69 period.)

At the third plenum of the Eleventh Central Committee, Chen was catapulted back onto the Politburo and its standing committee. Also, he was named first secretary of the Central Commission for Inspecting Party Discipline, created to restore the Party's organizational vitality. In mid-1979 he was also named a vice premier, but gave up the post a year later as part of an effort to elevate younger officials. Formally, he ranks number five in the Party hierarchy, but his role in economic and Party affairs has grown substantially since his return.

Hua Guofeng (Hua Kuo-feng), Party Vice Chairman

Born in 1920 or 1921 in Shanxi Province, Hua worked in his home county during the anti-Japanese and civil wars, and was subsequently assigned to a military unit that occupied Mao Zedong's native province of Hunan. In the early 1950s he served as Party secretary at the county and special district level, and achieved local prominence for his vigorous sponsorship of the agricultural collectivization movement. In 1958 Hua became a provincial vice governor and a member of the provincial Party committee, with responsibilities at various times for culture, education, finance and trade, and relations with non-Party groups. He survived the Cultural Revolution to become a vice chairman of the Hunan revolutionary committee in 1968 and first Party secretary in 1970.

Hua was transferred to Beijing in 1971, working initially in the State Council staff office under Zhou Enlai and on a special body investigating the Lin Biao affair. He was elected to the Politburo in 1973 and became a vice premier and minister of public security in 1975. His responsibilities at that time also included agriculture and science and technology.

After the death of Zhou Enlai in January 1976, Hua was named acting premier, leapfrogging the two most prominent contenders, Deng Xiaoping and Zhang Chunqiao. After Deng's purge in April 1976, Hua became premier and first vice chairman of the Party Central Committee, reportedly on Mao's proposal. Following Mao's death in September, the "gang of four" sought to block Hua's accession to the Party chairmanship. He played an important role in their arrest in October, and the Politburo named him chairman of the Party's Central Committee and Military Commission. He was the first person in PRC history to hold simultaneously the positions of Party chairman and premier.

But the very fact that Hua was Mao's chosen successor made him the target of Deng Xiaoping and other victims of the Cultural Revolution. After 1977 Deng successfully advocated policies, personnel changes, and evaluations of the past that went against the Maoist grain. Increasingly isolated, Hua's own political position deteriorated markedly during 1980. February saw the purge of four Politburo members (Wang Dongxing, Chen Xilian, Ji Dengkui, and Wu De) who, like Hua, had had close ties to Mao and rose during the Cultural Revolution. In September Hua gave up the post of premier to Zhao Ziyang. Under fire for "leftist" mistakes and fostering a "cult of personality," Hua resigned his top Party posts at the end of the year. It was formally announced in late June 1981 that Hu Yaobang was the new Party chairman and that Hua was to be a vice chairman.

FULL MEMBERS (in alphabetical order)

Chen Yonggui (Ch'en Yung-kui)

Chen was born in the 1910s. For many years he was the leader of the Dazhai production brigade in Shanxi Province, formerly the national model in agriculture. After serving as a county and provincial leader during the Cultural Revolution, Chen was elected to the Politburo in 1973 and became a vice premier in 1975. He made one of the major speeches at a conference on agricultural mechanization in December 1976.

Since 1979, Chen Yonggui and Dazhai have fallen on hard times. Deng Xiaoping and his colleagues prefer to spur food production by material incentives instead of Dazhai-type mobilization techniques. Also, attacking

Chen has been a way of weakening his ally Hua Guofeng. The final blow came in 1980 when it was charged that Dazhai had achieved its erstwhile model status by fabricating statistics. Chen was forced to resign his vice premiership in September of that year, and few observers expect him to remain on the Politburo for very long.

Deng Yingchao (Teng Ying-ch'ao)

Deng is the widow of former Premier Zhou Enlai. She was born in 1903, and is a revolutionary figure in her own right. Deng participated in the Long March and has always been an advocate of women's rights. During the late 1930s and early 1940s, she and Zhou were part a Communist liaison group in the Nationalists' capital of Chongqing. After 1949 Deng specialized in social welfare policy, but her position was largely honorific, especially in the 1960s. She weathered the Cultural Revolution well, and in the 1970s played an active role in the National People's Congress, serving as a vice chairman and member of its standing committee. In December 1978 she rose to Politburo status and was named second secretary of the Central Commission for Inspecting Discipline. Since Mao's death she has traveled widely in Asia, trying to bolster China's image and offset Soviet gains in the region.

Fang Yi (Fang Yi)

Born in 1916, Fang's experience in administrative and economic affairs dates back to 1939. Between 1949 and 1953 he served in various posts in Fujian, Shanghai, and the east China region. He was transferred to Beijing in September 1953 and served for a year as vice minister of finance. Between 1956 and 1960 Fang served in Hanoi as the representative of the ministry of foreign trade. Upon returning to China, his principal position was director of the commission for economic relations with foreign countries. Fang survived the Cultural Revolution, and returned to head the commission in January 1975.

Two years later he was transferred from economic affairs to science administration, becoming vice president of the Chinese Academy of Sciences. He was elected to the Politburo at the Eleventh Party Congress (August 1977) and became a vice premier at the Fifth National People's Congress in early 1978. He is concurrently the minister in charge of the state scientific and technological commission. Though named president of the Chinese Academy of Sciences in mid-1979, Fang resigned the post two years later, on the grounds that it should be held by a scientist rather than a government official.

Geng Biao (Keng Piao)

Geng is a native of Hunan Province, born in 1909. His career has swung from military affairs to diplomacy and back to the military. Geng was an army officer for most of the revolutionary period and a veteran of the Long March. After 1949 he specialized in foreign affairs, serving as ambassador to Sweden, Denmark, Finland, Pakistan, and Burma, as well as vice minister of foreign affairs between 1960 and 1963. From 1971 to 1979 Geng was director of the Party's international liaison department, responsible for relations with other Communist parties.

It has been during the post-Mao ascendancy of Deng Xiaoping that Geng has moved back into the military area. He was elected to the Politburo at the Eleventh Party Congress (August 1977) and in early 1978 became a vice premier. One year later he became secretary general (chief executive officer) of the Party's Military Commission, the highest policy-making body on defense issues. Geng served as host for US Defense Secretary Harold Brown in January 1980 and visited Washington four months later, the first high-level military exchanges between the two countries in thirty years. Geng became minister of national defense in March 1981, replacing the ailing Xu Xiangqian.

Li Desheng (Li Te-sheng)

A major beneficiary of the Cultural Revolution whose career has been in a holding pattern for some years now. Before 1966 he was commander of an army unit stationed in Anhui Province. Because of his early support of some of the more radical Red Guard groups in the province, Li became commander of the provincial military district in December 1967 and chairman of the provincial revolutionary committee in April 1968. He was named an alternate Politburo member in 1969 and transferred to Beijing the following year to become director of the general political department of the PLA, responsible for fostering ideological purity in the military.

Li's career peaked in 1973 when he became a full Politburo member and Party vice chairman. Then, late in the year, he was rotated out of Beijing, replacing Chen Xilian as commander of the Shenyang Military Region, his current post. Li lost his Party vice chairmanship in 1975, perhaps because of his ties to radical elements, but he has remained on the Politburo. Clearly though, his role is much diminished from that of 1973.

Liu Bocheng (Liu Po-ch'eng)

Born in 1892, Liu is one of the Party's veteran military commanders. He was on the Long March, and in the 1940s was commander of the Second Field Army, with Deng Xiaoping as his political commissar. After 1949 Liu became a member of the Party's Miltary Commission and director of the training department of the PLA until the unit's abolition in 1957. He has been a Politburo member since 1956 and a Military Commission vice chairman. Now in his late eighties, Liu is believed to be in very poor health.

Ni Zhifu (Ni Chih-fu)

The worker representative on the Politburo, Ni is believed to be in his middle to late forties. Raised in Shanghai, Ni moved to Beijing soon after 1949 to work at a machine tool plant where he became a worker technician. Ni was active during the Cultural Revolution, and was a municipal official in Beijing from 1971 to 1976. He became an alternate member of the Politburo in 1973. After the fall of the "gang of four" in late 1976, Ni worked in their old balliwick of Shanghai. He was raised to full Politburo membership at the Eleventh Party Congress in August 1977, and was transferred backed to Beijing late in the year. Ni is also chairman of the national federation of trade unions. Despite recent allegations of links with the leftist leaders of that period, his political position seems relatively secure.

Nie Rongzhen (Nieh Jung-chen)

Nie, born in 1899, is a native of Sichuan. A veteran of the Long March, he was commander of the North China Field Army in the late 1940s. He served as mayor of Beijing in the early 1950s, after which he was acting chief-of-staff of the PLA until 1954. Around the late 1950s he was named a vice chairman of the Party's Military Commission.

In the mid-1950s Nie began to specialize in military science administration. He became a vice premier 1956 and chairman of the scientific planning commission in 1957. Although that body was abolished during the Cultural Revolution, it is likely that Nie has continued to have some responsibility for scientific matters, possibly through the national defense commission for science and technology. Nie served on the Politburo briefly at the beginning of the Cultural Revolution, but was criticized during the Red Guard movement and lost his formal posts. He was restored to the Military Commission in 1974 and returned to the Politburo at the Eleventh Party Congress (August 1977).

Peng Chong (P'eng Ch'ung)

Peng, born in 1915, worked as a provincial and municipal official in Fujian and Jiangsu Provinces. He was the mayor of Nanjing before the Cultural Revolution, and assumed high positions in the government, Party, and military hierarchies of Jiangsu Province during the early 1970s. After the purge of the "gang of four," Peng was sent to Shanghai to stabilize the political situation there. Initially he held the post of third Party secretary, and was promoted to first secretary in late 1977. He was elected to the Politburo at the Eleventh Party Congress (August 1977). In the summer of 1979 he traveled to Western Europe. Since 1979 Peng's main problem has been political demands by large numbers of Shanghai natives, especially young people, who have been assigned to other parts of China and want to return home.

Peng Zhen (P'eng Chen)

Born in 1902, Peng is a long-time Party leader and was the first major purge victim of the Cultural Revolution. As early as 1943, he was head of the Party's powerful organization department, and was first elected to the Politburo in 1945. He became mayor of Beijing in 1951. In 1956 he was also named to the Party Secretariat, ranking immediately behind Deng Xiaoping.

On the eve of the Cultural Revolution, Peng was one of the strongest political figures in China, and some analysts speculated that he might succeed Mao Zedong. But this prediction proved erroneous: Peng was purged in May 1966 for protecting subordinates who had made thinly veiled attacks against Mao. In December of that year, he was personally subjected to humiliating criticism at a mass rally in Beijing.

Only in 1979, as the regime was openly rejecting the Cultural Revolution and restoring to power its principal victims, was Peng Zhen rehabilitated. He was named a vice chairman of the National People's Congress standing committee at mid-year and was elevated to the Politburo in September 1979. His main responsibility has been the development of the legal system.

Ulanhu (Ulanfu)

A Mongol, Ulanhu was born in 1906. From 1949 to 1966 he held the leading Party, government, and military key posts in Inner Mongolia. Concurrently, he was vice chairman and then chairman of the nationalities affairs commission of the State Council, and also a vice premier. In September 1956 he was named an alternate member of the Politburo. During the Cultural Revolution he was attacked by Red Guards and lost all his posts.

Ulanhu was rehabilitated in 1973, and was elected a full member of the Politburo at the Eleventh Party Congress in August 1977. Shortly before, it was revealed that he was also director of the Party's united front work department, responsible for Party relations with minority nationalities and with non-communist groups, particularly intellectuals.

Wang Zhen (Wang Chen)

Wang Zhen was born in 1909 in Mao Zedong's home province (Hunan) and Hu Yaobang's home county. He was on the Long March and spent much of his subsequent career as an army officer. Wang made a name for himself during the anti-Japanese war by having his troops engage in productive labor both to help the civilian populace and meet their own logistic requirements. From the early 1950s to the start of the Cultural Revolution, Wang was head of the railway corps of the PLA and minister of state farms and land reclamation. He became a vice premier in 1975, and a Politburo member at the December 1978 third plenum of the Eleventh Central Committee. He resigned his vice premiership in September 1980.

Wei Guoqing (Wei Kuo-ch'ing)

Born around 1914, Wei is a native of Guangxi Autonomous Region, a member of the Zhuang minority, and a veteran of the Long March. He became governor of Guangxi in 1955, and first Party secretary in 1961. Though heavily criticized by Red Guards during the Cultural Revolution, he held on to both his posts. He became a Politburo member in 1973. In October 1975, he was promoted to first Party secretary of Guangdong province. He was transferred to Beijing in Septmeber 1977 to serve as director of the PLA's general political department. On Deng Xiaoping's behalf he has worked to reduce the level of Maoist ideology in the military.

Xu Shiyou (Hsu Shih-yu)

In his mid-70s, Xu is a professional soldier who was on part of the Long March. He served as commander of the Nanjing Military Region from 1954 until 1973. Active in Jiangsu Province during the Cultural Revolution, Xu became chairman of that province's revolutionary committee in 1968 and first Party secretary in 1971. He was elected to the Politburo in 1969. During a rotation of regional military commanders in late 1973, Xu became commander of the Guangzhou Military Region, and so gave up his civil posts in Jiangsu. Reportedly, he was a strong supporter of Deng Xiaoping and a vocal advocate of Deng's 1977 rehabilitation. Xu played a major role in

China's February 1979 "punitive" expedition against Vietnam. One year later Xu left his Guangzhou post and was apparently working in Beijing.

Xu Xiangqian (Hsu Hsiang-ch'ien)

Born in 1902, Xu is known primarily for his distinguished military career before 1949. He participated in part of the Long March and, after war with Japan broke out in 1937 he had command responsibilities in the Eighth Route Army. In the late 1940s, he was a commander in the North China Field Army, led by Nie Rongzhen. After 1949, Xu was named chief-of-staff of the PLA but apparently never served actively in the position because of ill health (Nie acted in his stead). Like Nie, Xu was on the Politburo briefly during the Cultural Revolution. He was reelected at the Eleventh Party Congress (August 1977), and became minister of national defense and a vice premier in early 1978. Because of his health he resigned both posts in September 1980. He is still a vice chairman of the Party's Military Commission.

Yu Qiuli (Yu Ch'iu-li)

Born in 1912, Yu served as an army officer before 1949 and made a gradual transition into economic affairs thereafter. Immediately after the civil war Yu was part of the military occupation forces in both the northwest and southwest. In the mid-1950s he was transferred to Beijing to serve as director of the finance department of the PLA, and shortly thereafter became political commissar of the PLA's general logistics department.

In 1958 he moved out of the army to become minister of petroleum, spending much of the early 1960s opening up the Daqing oil field. In 1965 he was appointed a vice chairman of the state planning commission, and was one of the few ministers to receive Mao's repeated praise. Although he was severely criticized during the Cultural Revolution, Yu survived to become chairman of the state planning commission in October 1972. He became a vice premier in January 1975 and a Politburo member at the Eleventh Party Congress (August 1977).

In 1980 Yu came under attack as a leader of the "petroleum kingdom," a group of economic planners who allegedly overemphasized the role of oil in China's economic development. Yu lost his post at the state planning commission and was made head of the newly created and less prestigious state energy commission.

Zhang Tingfa (Chang T'ing-fa)

Zhang is a relative newcomer to top-level Party leadership. A professional air force officer, Zhang was named deputy chief-of-staff of the air force in 1958 and then promoted to become deputy commander in 1964. Dismissed during the Cultural Revolution at the time when Lin Biao's supporters dominated the air force, Zhang was rehabilitated as deputy air force commander in July 1975. He became air force commander in April 1977 and first secretary of the air force Party committee at about the same time. He replaced Ma Ning, who reportedly had connections to the "gang of four." Zhang became a Politburo member in August 1977, even though he had never been a member of the Central Committee. He is a member of the Party's Military Commission.

ALTERNATE MEMBERS

Chen Muhua (Ch'en Mu-hua)

Most of Chen's career has been spent in the commission/ministry of economic relations with foreign countries. A middle-level official at the start of the Cultural Revolution, she rose to vice minister in April 1971 and minister in 1977. Chen became an alternate member of the Politburo at the Eleventh Party Congress (August 1977), and became a vice premier in 1978, the only woman to hold that rank. She is one of two women on the Politburo, the other being Deng Yingchao. In recent years Chen has been responsible for the government's work in family planning, and in March 1981 was named head of a newly created state commission for that field.

Seypidin (Saifudin)

A Uighur, Seypidin is one of three minority members of the Politburo. (The others are Wei Guoqing and Ulanhu.) Born in 1915, Seypidin studied in the Soviet Union, and was actually a member of the Communist Party of the Soviet Union until he transferred his membership to the Chinese Party in 1950. He held leading Party, government, and military posts in Xinjiang from 1949 until the start of the Cultural Revolution, and was rehabilitated as early as 1968. He became first secretary in the early 1970s. He was elected an alternate member of the Politburo in 1973 and retained that position at the Eleventh Party Congress (August 1977). He lost his posts in Xinjiang in late 1977, probably because of links to the "gang of four," but remained a Politburo alternate, at least nominally.

Appendix B:
Documents on
US–China Relations

THE SHANGHAI COMMUNIQUE, FEBRUARY 27, 1972

. . . The leaders of the People's Republic of China and the United States of America found it beneficial to have this opportunity, after so many years without contact, to present candidly to one another their views on a variety of issues. They reviewed the international situation in which important changes and great upheavals are taking place and expounded their respective positions and attitudes.

The US side stated: Peace in Asia and peace in the world require efforts both to reduce immediate tensions and to eliminate the basic causes of conflict. The United States will work for a just and secure peace: just, because it fulfills the aspirations of peoples and nations for freedom and progress; secure, because it removes the danger of foreign aggression. The United States supports individual freedom and social progress for all the peoples of the world, free of outside pressure or intervention. The United States believes that the effort to reduce tensions is served by improving communication between countries that have different ideologies so as to lessen the risks of confrontation through accident, miscalculation or misunderstanding. Countries should treat each other with mutual respect and be willing to compete peacefully, letting performance be the ultimate judge. No country should claim infallibility and each country should be prepared to reexamine its own attitudes for the common good. . . .

The Chinese side stated: Wherever there is oppression, there is resistance. Countries want independence, nations want liberation and the people want revolution--this has become the irresistible trend of history. All nations, big or small, should be equal; big nations should not bully the small and strong nations should not bully the weak. China will never be a superpower and it opposes hegemony and power politics of any kind. The

Chinese side stated that it firmly supports the struggles of all the oppressed people and nations for freedom and liberation and that the people of all countries have the right to choose their social systems according to their own wishes and the right to safeguard the independence, sovereignty and territorial integrity of their own countries and oppose foreign aggression, interference, control and subversion. All foreign troops should be withdrawn to their own countries. . . .

There are essential differences between China and the United States in their social systems and foreign policies. However, the two sides agreed that countries, regardless of their social systems, should conduct their relations on the principles of respect for the sovereignty and territorial integrity of all states, nonaggression against other states, noninterference in the internal affairs of other states, equality and mutual benefit, and peaceful coexistence. International disputes should be settled on this basis, without resorting to the use or threat of force. The United States and the People's Republic of China are prepared to apply these principles to their mutual relations.

With these principles of international relations in mind the two sides stated that:

Progress toward the normalization of relations between China and the United States is in the interests of all countries;

Both wish to reduce the danger of international military conflict;

Neither should seek hegemony in the Asia-Pacific region and each is opposed to efforts by any other country or group of countries to establish such hegemony; and

Neither is prepared to negotiate on behalf of any third party or to enter into agreements or understandings with the other directed at other states.

Both sides are of the view that it would be against the interests of the peoples of the world for any major country to collude with another against other countries, or for major countries to divide up the world into spheres of interest.

The two sides reviewed the long-standing serious disputes between China and the United States. The Chinese side reaffirmed its position: The Taiwan question is the crucial question obstructing the normalization of relations between China and the United States; the Government of the People's Republic of China is the sole legal government of China; Taiwan is a province of China which has long been returned to the motherland; the liberation of Taiwan is China's internal affair in which no other country has the right to interfere; and all US forces and military installations must be withdrawn from Taiwan. The Chinese Government firmly opposes any activities which aim at the creation of "one China, one

Taiwan," "one China, two governments," "two Chinas," and "independent Taiwan" or advocate that "the status of Taiwan remains to be determined."

The US side declared: The United States acknowledges that all Chinese on either side of the Taiwan Strait maintain there is but one China and that Taiwan is a part of China. The United States Government does not challenge that position. It reaffirms its interest in a peaceful settlement of the Taiwan question by the Chinese themselves. With this prospect in mind, it affirms the ultimate objective of the withdrawal of all US forces and military installations from Taiwan. In the meantime, it will progressively reduce its forces and military installations on Taiwan as the tension in the area diminishes.

The two sides agreed that it is desirable to broaden the understanding between the two peoples. To this end, they discussed specific areas in such fields as science, technology, culture, sports and journalism, in which people-to-people contacts and exchanges would be mutually beneficial. Each side undertakes to facilitate the further development of such contacts and exchanges.

Both sides view bilateral trade as another area from which mutual benefit can be derived, and agreed that economic relations based on equality and mutual benefit are in the interest of the peoples of the two countries. They agree to facilitate the progressive development of trade between their two countries.

The two sides agreed that they will stay in contact through various channels, including the sending of a senior US representative to Peking from time to time for concrete consultations to further the normalization of relations between the two countries and continue to exchange views on issues of common interest.

The two sides expressed the hope that the gains achieved during this visit would open up new prospects for the relations between the two countries. They believe that the normalization of relations between the two countries is not only in the interest of the Chinese and American peoples but also contributes to the relaxation of tension in Asia and the world.

Source: Excerpted from Peking Review, March 3, 1972, pp. 4-5.

NORMALIZATION OF US-CHINA RELATIONS, DECEMBER 15-16, 1978

The Joint Communique

The United States of America and the People's Republic of China have agreed to recognize each other and to establish diplomatic relations as of January 1, 1979.

The United States of America recognizes the Government of the People's Republic of China as the sole legal government of China. Within this context, the people of the Unites States will maintain cultural, commercial, and other unofficial relations with the people of Taiwan.
The United States of America and the People's Republic of China reaffirm the principles agreed on by the two sides in the Shanghai communique and emphasize once again that:
--Both wish to reduce the danger of international military conflict.
--Neither should seek hegemony in the Asia-Pacific region or in any other region of the world and each is opposed to efforts by any other country or group of countries to establish such hegemony.
--Neither is prepared to negotiate on behalf of any third party or to enter into agreements or understandings with the other directed at other states.
--The Government of the United States of America acknowledges the Chinese position that there is but one China and Taiwan is a part of China.
--Both believe that normalization of relations is not only in the interest of the Chinese and American peoples but also contributes to the cause of peace in Asia and the world.
The United States of America and the People's Republic of China will exchange ambassadors and establish embassies on March 1, 1979.

The United States' Statement

As of January 1, 1979, the United States of America recognizes the People's Republic of China as the sole legal government of China. On the same date, the People's Republic of China accords similar recognition to the United States of America. The United States thereby establishes diplomatic relations with the People's Republic of China.
On that same date, January 1, 1979, the United States of America will notify Taiwan that it is terminating diplomatic relations and that the mutual defense treaty between the United States and the Republic of China is being terminated in accordance with the provisions of the treaty. The United States also states that it will be withdrawing its remaining military personnel from Taiwan within four months.
In the future, the American people and the people of Taiwan will maintain commercial, cultural, and other relations without official government representation and without diplomatic relations.
The Administration will seek adjustments to our laws and regulations to permit the maintenance of commercial, cultural, and other nongovernmental relationships in the

new circumstances that will exist after normalization. The United States is confident that the people of Taiwan face a peaceful and prosperous future. The United States continues to have an interest in the peaceful resolution of the Taiwan issue and expects that the Taiwan issue will be settled peacefully by the Chinese people themselves.

The United States believes that the establishment of diplomatic relations with the People's Republic will contribute to the welfare of the American people, to the stability of Asia where the United States has major security and economic interests and to the peace of the entire world.

China's Statement

As of January 1, 1979, the People's Republic of China and the United States of America recognize each other and establish diplomatic relations, thereby ending the prolonged abnormal relationship between them. This is an historic event in Sino-United States relations.

As is known to all, the Government of the People's Republic of China is the sole legal government of China and Taiwan is a part of China. The question of Taiwan was the crucial issue obstructing the normalization of relations between China and the United States. It has now been resolved between the two countries in the spirit of the Shanghai communique and through their joint efforts, thus enabling the normalization of relations so ardently desired by the people of the two countries.

As for the way of bringing Taiwan back to the embrace of the motherland and reunifying the country, it is entirely China's internal affair.

At the invitation of the U.S. Government, Teng Hsiao-p'ing, Deputy Prime Minister of the State Council of the People's Republic of China, will pay an official visit to the United States in January 1979, with a view to further promoting the friendship between the two peoples and good relations between the two countries.

Source: Peking Review, December 22, 1978, pp. 8-12.

TAIWAN RELATIONS ACT OF 1979

Declaration of Policy

. . . Sec. 2. (b) It is the policy of the United States--
(1) to preserve and promote extensive, close, and friendly commercial, cultural, and other relations between the United States and the people on Taiwan, as well as the people on the China mainland and all other

peoples of the Western Pacific area;
(2) to declare that peace and stability in the area are in the political, security, and economic interests of the United States, and are matters of international concern;
(3) to make clear that the United States decision to establish diplomatic relations with the People's Republic of China rests upon the expectation that the future of Taiwan will be determined by peaceful means;
(4) to consider any effort to determine the future of Taiwan by other than peaceful means, including by boycotts or embargoes, a threat to the peace and security of the Western Pacific area and of grave concern to the United States;
(5) to provide Taiwan with arms of a defensive character; and
(6) to maintain the capacity of the United States to resist any resort to force or other forms of coercion that would jeopardize the security, or the social or economic system, of the people on Taiwan.

(c) Nothing contained in this Act shall contravene the interest of the United States in human rights, especially with respect to the human rights of all the approximately eighteen million inhabitants of Taiwan. The preservation and enhancement of the human rights of all the people on Taiwan are hereby reaffirmed as objectives of the United States.

Implementation of US Policy with Regard to Taiwan

Sec. 3. (a) In furtherance of the policy set forth in section 2 of this Act, the United States will make available to Taiwan such defense articles and defense services in such a quantity as may be necessary to enable Taiwan to maintain a sufficient self-defense capability.

(b) The President and the Congress shall determine the nature and the quantity of such defense articles and services based solely upon their judgment of the needs of Taiwan, in accordance with procedures established by law. Such determination of Taiwan's defense needs shall include review by the United States military authorities in connection wiith recommendations to the President and Congress.

(c) The President is directed to inform Congress promptly of any threat to the security or the social or economic system of the people of Taiwan and any danger to the interests of the United States arising therefrom. The President and the Congress shall determine, in accordance with constitutional process, appropriate action by the United States in response to any such danger.

Application of Laws

Sec. 4. (a) The absence of diplomatic relations shall not affect the application of the laws of the United States with respect to Taiwan, and the laws of the United States shall apply with respect to Taiwan in the manner that the laws of the United States applied with respect to Taiwan prior to January 1, 1979. . . .

The American Institute in Taiwan

Sec. 6. (a) Programs, transactions, and other relations conducted or carried out by the President or any other agency of the United States Government with respect to Taiwan shall, in the manner and to the extent directed by the President, be conducted and carried out by and through--
(1) The American Institute in Taiwan ["Institute" hereafter], a nonprofit corporation incorporated under the laws of the District of Columbia, or
(2) such comparable successor nongovernmental entity as the President may designate. . . .

(b) Whenever the President or any agency of the United States Government is authorized or required by or pursuant to the laws of the United States to enter into, perform, enforce, or have in force an agreement or transaction relative to Taiwan, such agreement or transaction shall be entered into, peformed, and enforced, in the manner and extent directed by the President, by or through the Institute.
(c) To the extent that any law, rule, regulation, or ordinance of the District of Columbia, or of any State or political subdivision theeof in which the Institute is incorporated or doing business, impedes or otherwise interferes with the performance of the functions of the Institute pursuant to this Act, such law, rule, regulation, or ordinance shall be deemed to be prempted by this Act. . . .

Taiwan Instrumentality

Sec. 10. (a) Whenever the President or any agency of the United States Government is authorized or required by or pursuant to the laws of the United States to render or provide to or receive or accept from Taiwan, any performance, communication, assurance, undertaking, or other action, such action shall, in the manner and extent directed by the President, be rendered or provided to, or received or accepted from, an instrumentality established by Taiwan which the President determines has the necessary authority under the laws applied by the people on Taiwan to provide assurances and to take other actions on

behalf of Taiwan in accordance with the Act.
(b) The President is requested to extend to the instrumentality established by Taiwan the same number of offices and complement of personnel as were previously operated in the United States by the governing authorities on Taiwan recognized as the Republic of China prior to January 1, 1979.
(c) Upon the granting by Taiwan of comparable privileges and immunities with respect to the Institute and its appropriate personnel, the President is authorized to extend with respect to the Taiwan instrumentality and its appropriate personnel, such privileges and immunities (subject to appropriate conditions and obligations) as may be necessary for the effective performance of their functions. . . .

Definitions

Sec. 15. For the purposes of this Act--
(1) the term "laws of the United States" includes any statute, rule, regulation, ordinance, order, or judicial rule of decision of the United States or any political subdivision thereof; and
(2) the term "Taiwan" includes, as the context may require, the islands of Taiwan and the Pescadores (Penghu), the people on those islands, corporations and other entities and associations created or organized under the laws applied on those islands, and the governing authorities on Taiwan recognized by the United States as the Republic of China prior to January 1, 1979, and any successor governing authorities (including political subdivisions, agencies, and instrumentalities thereof). . . .

Source: Public Law No. 96-8, 93 Stat. 14.

STATEMENT OF SECRETARY OF STATE HAIG ON US CHINA POLICY, MARCH 16, 1981

. . . [President Reagan] visualizes continued efforts to normalize our relationship with the People's Republic of China. This is a fundamental strategic reality and a strategic imperative. It is of overriding importance to international stability and world peace. He also visualizes adherence to the communique associated with the normalization agreement with [Beijing]. And he visualizes a non-official status with the people of Taiwan, based on adherence to American law established in the Taiwan Relations Act. . . . We do not view these-- the communique and the act--as mutually exclusive."

Source: Time, March 16, 1981.

Appendix C:
A Statistical Profile of Chinese Economic Development

	1957	1978	1979	1980
Revenues and Expenditures (billions of yuan)				
Government Revenues	31.0	112.1	106.8	108.0
Government Investment	12.6	39.5	39.5	28.1
Government Health, Education, Science, and Welfare Expenditures	4.6	11.3	13.2	14.8$_P$
Military Expenditures	5.5	16.8	22.3	19.3$_P$
Output Data				
Grain (MMT)	196	305	332	318
Fish Products (MMT)	3.12	4.66	4.305	4.497
Cotton (MMT)	1.64	2.167	2.207	2.71
Oil Seed Crops (MMT)	3.8	4.6	5.641	7.691
Sugar (MMT)	.864	2.267	2.5	2.57
Bicycles (thousands)	806	8,540	10,090	13,020
Sewing Machines (thousands)	278	4,865	5,870	7,680
Crude Steel (MMT)	5.4	31.8	34.48	37.12
Petroleum (MMT)	1.5	104.1	106.15	105.92
Electric Power (billion KW hrs.)	19.3	256.6	281.95	300.6
Transport				
Freight Turnover (bill. ton kms)	173	939	1042	1202
Commerce				
Retail Sales (billion yuan)	47.4	152.75	175.25	214

Education Enrollments
(thousands)

University and College	441	850	1,020	1444
Technical Secondary Schools	778	880	1,199	1243
Secondary Schools	6,281	65,480	59,050	55,081
Primary Schools	64,279	146,240	146,630	146,270

Health

Hospital Beds (thousands)	364	1,856	1,932	1982

Source: Chinese State Statistical Bureau and other Chinese sources.

Notes: Revenue and expenditure data are in current prices. Grain output, under Chinese definition, is measured in unprocessed weight, and includes tubers, pulses, and soybeans. Oil seed crops include only peanuts, rape seed, and sesame seed. P = planned level; MMT = millions of metric tons.

Index

Academic Exchanges
   US-China, 86-87
Agriculture, 41, 42, 44
Alienation
   political, 19-20, 53, 56, 59
Anti-Confucianism and families, 69
Arms sale
   to Taiwan by US, 88-89
Art
   policy toward, 33-35

Banking system, 48, 49
Baoshan steel complex, 22, 32
Birth control, 72, 76, 105
Brown, Harold, 80-82, 100
Brezhnev, Leonid, 83
Brzezinski, Zbigniew, 80
Budget deficit, 41, 44
Bureaucratism, 15, 23-24
   and youth, 55, 63-64
Bush, George, 88
Byrd, Robert, 88

Career management of youth, 64, 66
Carter, Jimmy, 82
   See also US China policy, Carter administration
Central economic planning, 41-42, 47-48, 48, 51
Chen Muhua, 105
Chen Xilian, 30
Chen Yonggui, 25, 29-30, 32, 98-99
Chen Yun, 25, 97
Chinese attitudes towards the US, 90
Chinese Communist Party
   current problems of, 15, 19-20, 23-25, 64-65
   Deng Xiaoping's vision of, 15
   Hu Yaobang's vision of, 15
   policies towards rural areas, 69-72
   reform measures, 15-16, 20-21
   separation from state, 25-27
"Class Counselor," 59
Cline, Ray, 89
Collective agriculture and families, 70, 76
Collective enterprises, 55, 58-59, 75
Communist Youth League, 10-11, 59
Consular affairs agreement
   US-China, 85
Consumer goods, 42
   and foreign trade, 46-48
Corruption, 23-24, 66, 75
Crime, 19-20, 59
Criminal justice system, 23, 35-36, 102
Crisis of faith, 19-20, 66
Criticism of officials, 22-23

Cultural expression
  policies toward, 33-35
Cultural Revolution, 36
  evaluation of, 11, 13,
    95, 102
  Mao and 38-39
  rationale for, 10,
    28-29, 95
  youth and, 56

Daqing oil field, 104
Dazhai production brigade,
  98-99
  criticism of, 29-30
Decentralization
  economic, 41-42, 49-50
"Democracy Wall," 32, 56,
  59
Demographic trends, 74-75
Deng Xiaoping, 4, 12, 19,
  23, 24, 29, 32, 33,
  36-37, 38, 39, 40, 89,
  90, 94-95, 97, 98, 99,
  100, 101, 103
  and Hu Yaobang, 7-8,
    9-10, 12
  on the Party, 15
  resistance to, 18
Deng Yingchao, 99, 105
Dissidence, 32-33, 57

Economic reform
  See "Restructuring"
Education, 54, 57-58, 60,
  64-65, 66, 74-75
Elections, 20-23, 66
Employment, 44, 54-55,
  58-59, 64, 66, 74-75
Energy supplies, 43
Enterprise management, 49
"Evenhandedness," 80-83
Export processing zones,
  46-47
Export promotion, 49-50

Family
  and anti-Confucianism,
    69
  and collective agri-
    culture, 70, 76
  and demographic trends,
    74
  as household, 67-68,
    72-74
  as kinship group, 68,
    75
  economic role, 70, 72-73
  impact on four moderni-
    zations, 74-77
  in 1949, 68-69
  loyalty to, 67, 75,
    76-77
  migration restrictions
    and, 71-72, 73
  revival after 1949, 69
  rural, 68, 70-72, 75-76
  socialization by, 74, 75
  urban, 68-69, 72-74
  welfare role, 71, 72, 74
Family planning, 72, 76,
  105
Fang Yi, 99
"Feudal Patriarchy," 24-25
Film festival
  US-China 87
"Foolish Old Man," 30
Ford, Gerald, 89
Foreign economic
  relations, 85-86
Foreign presence in China,
  60, 62, 87,
Foreign trade
  and economic system,
    47-48
  approach to, 45-46
  measures in 1980, 46-47
  performance in 1980, 47
"Four Bigs," 33
Fu Yuehua, 32

GATT, 47
Geng Biao, 82, 100

Haig, Alexander, 79, 89
Harsch, Joseph, 83
Holbrooke, Richard, 82
Households, 67-68
  economic role of, 69-70,
    72-73
Hu Yaobang, 39-40, 93-94,
    95, 98
  and Hua Guofeng, 7-8,
    13-14, 32
  and Deng Xiaoping, 7-8,
    9-10, 12, 13-14
  and Party reform, 15-16

Hu Yaobang (cont.)
  career to 1949, 8-9
  career, 1949-66, 10-11
  career, post-1977, 11-12
  control of Party, 13
  current tasks, 7-8,
    14-16
  evaluation of Mao, 13,
    29
  on role of Party, 15-16,
    20
  personality, 16
Hua Guofeng, 19, 22, 23,
    27, 29, 39-40, 82, 94,
    95, 97-98, 99
  and Hu Yaobang, 7-8, 13
  criticism of, 14, 30-32
  resigns premiership, 25
Hunan province
  revolutionary activity
    in, 8

Idealistic youth, 62
Import substitution, 46,
    47
Industrial management, 45,
    47-48
Industry
  structure of, 48
Inflation, 41, 44, 50-51
International Monetary
    Fund, 41, 47, 85
Investment
  See "Readjustment"

Ji Dengkui, 30
Jiang Qing, 35, 37, 38, 39

Kinship group, 68, 75

Labor productivity, 45
Li Desheng, 100
Li Xiannian, 25, 96-97
Lin Biao, 11, 35-38, 105
Literature
  policy toward, 33-35
Liu Bocheng, 25, 101
Liu Shaoqi, 10, 28-29, 37,
    38, 95
Liu Xinwu, 59
Liuyang county
  Party leaders from, 8-9
  revolution in, 8

Living standards, 41, 42,
    43
Legitimacy, 4-5, 17-20

Ma Ning, 105
Ma Tianshui, 39
Mainland-Taiwan relations,
    89
Management
  enterprise, 49, 51
  industrial, 45, 47-48
Mandatory retirement for
  officials, 24-25
Mao Yuanxin, 39
Mao Zedong, 7-8, 10-11,
    93-94, 95, 97, 102,
    104
  and Cultural Revolution,
    38-39
  and Hua Guofeng, 14,
    31-32
  evaluation of, 13, 15,
    18-19, 28-30
Maritime relations agree-
    ment
  US-China, 83, 84-85
Market socialism, 42,
    47-50
Marriage reform law, 69
Merit system for
    officials, 16, 25
Migration restrictions, 55
  and rural families,
    71-72
  and urban families, 73
Military
  discontent in, 27
  modernization of, 27, 80
Mondale, Walter, 80
Most-favored-nation
    status, 83

National People's Congress
  criticism of officials,
    22-23
  resignation of senior
    officials, 25-26
Ni Zhifu, 101
Nie Rongzhen, 25, 101, 104
Normalization documents,
    109-111
  Reagan administration
    and, 79

Participation
 political, 20-27, 66
Peasant youth, 62, 72
Peng Chong, 102
Peng Zhen, 102
People's Liberation Army
 discontent, 27
 modernization of, 27, 80
Perry, William, 82
"Petroleum Kingdom," 104
Policy toward youth, 65-66
Political alienation,
 19-20, 53, 56, 59
Political corruption, 15,
 23-24, 66, 75
Political dissidence, 32-33, 57
Political legitimacy, 4-5,
 17-20
Political participation,
 20-23, 66
Political reform, 15-16,
 17, 24-25
Political succession, 4,
 13-14, 25-27, 30-32
Population control, 72,
 76, 105
Price system, 48, 50
Product quality, 45
Productivity, 45
Protectionism, 46

"Readjustment," 41-42
 rationale for, 42
 results of, 42-43
Reagan, Ronald
 views on Taiwan issue,
 79, 87-88, 90-91
 PRC response to, 87-89
Red Guards, 55-57
 in universities, 56
 independent thinking of,
 57
 political activity, 57
 resettlement in countryside, 55-56
Reform
 economic: See
 "Restructuring"
Reform
 political, 15-16, 17,
 24-25
"Restructuring," 41-42,
 47-48, 49
 delay in, 51-52
Role models, 64-65
Rural families, 68
 after 1949, 70-72
 economic role of, 70, 76
 in 1949, 68
 strength of loyalties,
 75-76
 welfare role of, 71

"Self-reliance," 45-46, 47
"Sent-down" youth, 55-56,
 64, 66
Separation of Party and
 state, 25-27
Seypidin, 105
Shanghai Communique
 excerpts, 107-109
Social welfare
 rural families and, 71
 urban families and, 72
"Socialist democracy,"
 20-23
Socialization by families,
 74, 75
Song Renqiong, 9, 13
Soviet Union
 and US-China relations,
 80-83, 90
Standard of living, 41, 42
Succession
 political, 4, 13-14,
 25-27, 30-32
Swing youth group, 60,
 62-63
 government approach to,
 62
 job satisfaction of, 60

Taiwan
 Taiwan Relations Act,
 excerpts, 111-114
 relations with mainland,
 89
Taiwan Relations Act, 87,
 88
 excerpts, 111-114
Teenagers, 57-59
 and four modernizations,
 59
 crime by, 19-20, 59
 employment of, 58-59

Teenagers (cont.)
  in universities, 58
Textile agreements
  US-China, 47, 83, 84
  with EEC, 47
Trade
  US-China, 83
Trial of "Lin-Jiang
  cliques," 18-19, 35-39

Ulanhu, 102-103
Unemployment, 44, 75
US-China policy
  Carter administration,
    79, 80-87, 88-89
  Reagan administration,
    79, 89, 90-91, 112
US-China relations
  cultural, 86-87, 91
  economic, 83-86, 90-91
  military, 80-83, 90, 104
  political, 80-83, 90
  Soviet factor, 80-83, 90
  Taiwan issue, 87-90
  See also Shanghai Communique, Normalization Documents, Taiwan Relations Act
Universities, 56, 58
Urban families, 68
  after 1949, 68, 72-74
  economic role of, 72-73
  in 1949, 68-69
  welfare role of, 72

Vance, Cyrus, 80, 82

Wang Dongxing, 12, 30
Wang Hongwen, 35
Wang Lei, 24
Wang Renzhong, 25
Wang Zhen, 9, 25, 103
Wei Guoqing, 103
Wei Jingsheng, 32
Welfare
  and rural families, 72
  and urban families, 72
"What If I Were Real?", 65
Wolff, Lester, 82-83
Woodcock, Leonard, 88
Wu De, 30

Xiyang county, 32

  See also Dazhai
    production brigade
Xu Shiyou, 103-104
Xu Xiangqian, 25, 100, 104
Xue Muqiao, 51-52

Yang Yong, 9
Yao Wenyuan, 35, 38
Ye Jianying, 25, 94
Youth
  alienation of, 19-20,
    53-54
  and the four modernizations, 53-54,
    57, 59
  Chinese dimension of
    problem, 63-65
  crime, 19-20, 59
  cynicism of, 54
  discipline of, 54
  educational level, 54
  employment, 54-55,
    58-59, 64, 75
  former Red Guards,
    55-57
  government policy,
    65-66
  idealists, 62
  in Shanghai, 56-57, 102
  job satisfaction, 59,
    60, 75
  peasants, 62, 72
  swing group, 60, 61-63
  teenagers, 57-59
Youth League, 10-11, 59
Yu Qiuli, 104

Zhang Aiping, 27
Zhang Chunqiao, 35, 38
Zhang Guangdou, 90
Zhang Tingfa, 104-105
Zhao Ziyang, 25-26, 39-40,
  95-96, 98
Zhou Enlai, 7, 8, 11-12,
  36, 99